Johannes Hartl is a theologian
worship – and an inspiring visioi

God is our Loving Father, our very present help in trouble, our all in all. Sometimes life gets so busy, and we aren't quite sure how to engage with God even when we know he is real. In *Simply Pray*, Johannes Hartl will convince you to come away again to the secret place where God wants to share the whispers of his heart with you. If your prayer life has grown cold, take this chance to re-connect with the Source of everything … He is waiting for you!

DR. HEIDI BAKER
Founder, and CEO of Iris Global

Simply Pray is one of the most beautiful yet practical books on prayer I have read. Johannes captures the heart of devotion and the sense of our human desire to connect with the divine, but he takes it further by giving us some incredibly helpful tools to grow in our intimacy with God. I have read many great inspirational books on prayer, but some have left me with the question 'Yes, but how?' Johannes not only inspires devotion but also responds to that question with useful exercises and examples that work in our day to day lives. I believe this book will both inspire and assist you in learning to walk and talk with God.

BRIAN HEASLEY
International Prayer Director 24-7 Prayer

Johannes Hartl is a gifted storyteller – he creatively draws from his experience presenting popular themes as springboards for reflection and prayer. Each accessible chapter moves from his daily life through the word of God in order to teach us something about ourselves. Then we are invited and helped to go forward in prayer. This book will speak to people on many levels – it is inspirational, exhortational and full of practical tips. I recommend it for anyone who is seeking to go deeper in prayer.

MICHELLE MORAN
Co-founder of Sion Community for Evangelism and Leader within International Catholic Charismatic Renewal

Simply Pray gives us a fresh vision to encounter Jesus more consistently and to live every day in wonder of a life dedicated to prayer. Johannes Hartl inspires us to pursue prayer more passionately, and therefore know God more intimately even in the busyness of life.

MIKE BICKLE
Director, International House of Prayer of Kansas City

Simply Pray creatively invites us to encounter a good and joyful God at the everyday intersection of heaven's glory and the majestic mundane of earth.

ADAM COX
Founder and Lead Pastor, Navah Church KC; 24-7 Prayer USA and Global Communities Team

If you want to discover a deeper, richer lifestyle of prayer and experiencing God's presence, *Simply Pray* is a must read. It introduces practical, creative and challenging tools that equip a lifestyle of listening to the voice of God by learning how to tune out noisy distractions of everyday life. This book is especially transformational and liberating if you're someone who has a life filled with relationships and responsibilities.

LORI ROY
Director of Missions and Prayer, Heartland Community Church

If you want to walk with God, pick up this book. You were made to pray, it's in your design. But working out how to pray is another question, and it's exactly why this book exists. It's packed with experience and wisdom, as Johannes creatively intrigues, beautifully inspires and gently urges us into the adventure of relationship with God. Those who fall on their knees will land on their feet, so reading this book is an absolute must.

PETE WYNTER
Leadership Pastor, HTB and Founder, Onelife

Simple, profound and practical. There are many journeys in life, but the one that matters most is the one we're invited to take with God – deeper into his life and love. This book comes from the heart of someone who has gone far on that journey already and will help both those who are just starting out and those who are on the way but looking for encouragement to keep going.

PAUL HARCOURT
National Leader of New Wine England

SIMPLY
PRAY

SIMPLY PRAY

Twelve Steps to a
Transformed Life

JOHANNES HARTL

Muddy
Pearl

Published in 2018 by
Muddy Pearl, Edinburgh, Scotland.
www.muddypearl.com
books@muddypearl.com

The original German edition was published as Einfach Gebet
Copyright © 2016 SCM R. Brockhaus in der SCM Verlagsgruppe GmbH, 58452
Witten, Germany.
(www.scm-brockhaus.de)

British Library Cataloguing in Publication Data
A catalogue record for this book is available from the British Library
ISBN 978-1-910012-65-9
Cover design by Jeff Miller
Typeset in Minion by Revo Creative Ltd, Lancaster
Printed in Great Britain by Bell & Bain Ltd, Glasgow

CONTENTS

INTRODUCTION

THE JOURNEY OF YOUR LIFE

Life is more. And everyone, everywhere knows this. Life. To start with, life is what we can see and touch. Sunshine. Cars. Lasagne. Your right hand. The wind in your hair. People outside your window. The whole of life is full of things, people and happenings. True, this is just the visible, the tangible. All of this, I call 'the box'; it is the frame of meaning in which normal life plays out.

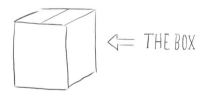

Animals eat, sleep and run around as well. And they are content, as a rule, as long as they have enough food and a mate for procreation. Humankind is a curious exception as the only living creature with this idea that there is something more. That there is a deeper meaning, a hidden secret, a higher dimension. This dimension is what this book is about – about the attempt to seize hold of these things and to enter into them, deeply. It gets really practical. Each chapter explores one more step into the invisible – into the great fascinating reality outside the box. So, here are twelve ideas for the adventure, the journey into a life that is not confined by the walls of the box.

But first, an apology: I am going to address you personally. I hope that is OK. As the author of this book, I will venture to take you, the reader, by the hand and to show you the steps I myself, day by day and for many years, have taken. In a personal and very simple way. And for this reason, I will presume to talk to you in a very direct way.

OUT OF THE BOX

Let's think about life. We are on this earth for a few decades and then it's over. Where do we come from? Where are we going? And what is the meaning of it all anyway? Questions that many people never ask, but which, when we are, one day, fully awake, will no longer be answered by cheap clichés. How can we find out where we have come from and why we exist?

It's only possible when …

Yes, when exactly?

Take a machine that you don't understand. Screws, levers, arms, springs – none of which give any indication of what it is for. You can touch it, watch it, listen to it. But what it actually is, is not automatically clear.

If you want to know how a mechanical appliance works properly, it is best to start with the question of what it was made for. For what purpose was it conceived? What purpose does it fulfil? You can only understand a machine when you know what it is there for. If there is any doubt, the creator knows best, because

it was he who thought up the device for that purpose. The same is true of humankind.

You are alive. Indeed, the fact that you exist is not because of fate or the will of your parents. The fact that your parents exist is only because there was someone before them. These are givens, facts, just like oxygen and gravity. So, where is it all from? The meaning of your own life, the meaning of the entire world, stands and falls with the same questions as the curious machine: why is there even anything, and not more nothing? And to what purpose? Here, the question of meaning points inevitably towards the question of the Creator. The Creator of men and women, and of the universe.

The reason behind absolutely everything reveals itself only if we come to know he who made everything. Yet by 'to know' I don't mean like by reading a book about him. Rather, I mean true, direct contact. And there is a skill to gaining this personal knowledge: it is called prayer. Prayer is not everything. But without prayer everything is nothing. And everything – yes, actually, everything in life changes if we begin to pray in earnest. That sounds like a cliché. And indeed it is one that, again and again in my own life, and in the lives of hundreds of other people that I am on this road with, proves to be true.

I write as someone personally affected. Since 2005, my wife Jutta and I have led the House of Prayer in Augsburg. 'Night and day we pray' is our slogan: with us prayer never ceases, by day or by night. 365 days a year, twenty-four hours a day. After all this time we definitely have one or two things to say about this exciting adventure with God. But this book is not about the House of Prayer, rather it is about normal daily life. All of the exercises in this book work in a completely average everyday life, not only in a monastery, or a House of Prayer or on a desert island.

PRAYER IS NOT EVERYTHING. BUT WITHOUT PRAYER EVERYTHING IS NOTHING.

There is a poignant instance in the Gospels when the disciples ask Jesus their Lord to explain something. What could that be? Did they want to learn from Jesus what the secret of his shining love was? Or the key to world peace? Or why he could heal the sick? For me personally, for example, there would have been a burning interest in why exactly Jesus had turned water into wine (as someone who likes a good glass of Bordeaux, I find this question truly helpful). And yet instead, the disciples asked for only one lesson. And that was: 'Teach us to pray.' Why this question, exactly? Clearly there was something in the prayer life of Jesus that was so compelling that the disciples simply had to get to the bottom of this secret. And clearly they saw in his life the significance and impact that prayer had on everything else that he did. He did nothing without prayer.

The answer Jesus gives is interesting: Jesus does indeed teach them to pray. He could have said, 'It isn't something that can be learned, it is a gift, you either have it or you don't.' That would then turn prayer into a character trait. Either someone is pious from birth, or is truly 'religiously unmusical'.[1] But no, prayer is evidently

1 In the words of Jürgen Habermas, speaking about himself in his speech to the German Book Trade Peace Prize 2001.

something that you can learn. And yet, even though the disciples were on the road with Jesus for such a long time, somehow or other they had apparently not spontaneously picked the skill up. Therefore, prayer is, very importantly, something that you *have to* learn. Something that you can grow in.

This book should help you to learn to pray. It is like a do-it-yourself course in one of the most important subjects in life, perhaps the most important of all. It is not a theory, rather it is to do with every aspect of existence, and therefore, how completely different this existence can become. The adventure of your life is waiting for you. The biggest challenge and the loveliest secret. And yet be warned: from now on, nothing will be the same again.

CHAPTER 1

NOTHING

NOTHING

My left trouser pocket feels peculiarly empty, because something is missing. I don't need to respond to anything, there is no need to worry that in the next few days something will buzz or ring. Because in my trouser pocket there is nothing. I have no mobile phone with me, no internet and no work to do. It feels almost like withdrawal. The last few days have been so full: talks, meetings, projects, decisions. I have been uprooted, torn away from so many matters that a few hours ago filled my thoughts. And now I have been sitting for half an hour in the car, all alone – and without the otherwise seemingly indispensable electronic equipment.

A first observant look out of the car window. May-green meadows rushing past, and suddenly the question: what does one even do here for a whole day if one is not a cow? Four days in Allgäu, far away from everything. Overcast sky, light rain. From village to village, in ever more rural parts. There is just so much of this landscape, stretching so far into the distance. So many villages with unknown names. Nothing much going on here. Nothing, evidently.

Only when the key turns in the lock and I set foot in the holiday home, does it hit me with full force: I will be here for four whole days. How had I become involved with such an idea? 'Simply do nothing, for once,' a good friend had advised. Hmmm. Interesting idea. But what exactly does 'nothing' mean? Just do some reading or writing? No, nothing. Think through my life goals? No, nothing. Go walking and enjoy nature a bit? Not that either. Excuse me? That's just not doable. Yet, something excites me. Yes. What might actually happen? Suddenly, I'm scared at the thought. Because it is so unfamiliar, especially to such an active person. Just do nothing? With no one? And no input? For me there is always something going on. And if nothing is going on, then I look for something to do. I am the kind of person who takes a pile of books to the beach. Who makes use of every moment of waiting time, at least to make some plans. To save the world, for example.

Yet, now I'm sitting on the sofa, staring into nothingness. It feels so unfamiliar. The silence seems almost thick enough to touch, and wraps itself around everything. Red, partially sunlit clouds in the early evening sky. The first hour passes. The honey-yellow of the evening light over the house opposite. The quietness almost hurts. No idea how I will bear four whole days. But who knows what there is still to discover? Somehow, I feel like Neil Armstrong must have felt when he took his first steps on the moon. Undiscovered terrain. And the idea that there could be something big waiting for me.

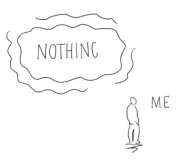

NOTHING

What is there actually, when nothing is happening? An appointment cancelled. A friend doesn't turn up. The work is finished more quickly than expected. There, where earlier there was an appointment on the calendar, is now only white paper.

What happens when nothing is going on? Usually we look for something to do. We put a pizza in the oven, do a little housework, write an email or simply turn on the TV. Because the silence, the nothingness, is strange. Headphones in the ears, quickly check Facebook, call someone up. Because to be alone is such a thing …
Why actually? Is there perhaps fear of the silence, of being alone? What would be so bad, if for once there was nothing? What would happen?

Most people spend their whole lives fleeing from nothingness, they get a shock when they are alone and there is nothing to do. It becomes crucial to quickly turn something on, eat something or drink something, watch something or do something – just not to come to rest. To run away. The problem is: sometime or other that will bring on the nothingness anyway. The yawning emptiness, opening up like a crater in front of our feet as soon as the front door clicks behind us; the morning after; the exhaustion after the big project. We just jump quickly to the next distraction. And then another task. And then another distraction. But that too will end. At some point the nothingness catches up with us all. Sometimes only when we are lying in the hospital. Or when we are struggling with burnout. A relationship breakdown. You start drawing your pension or the job is gone. Finally, on our deathbed, at least, there can be no more running away.

IF WE FACE THE NOTHINGNESS, A SILENT INVITATION SOUNDS IN EVERY MOMENT: 'STOP WITH THE RUNNING AWAY. THERE IS SO MUCH MORE TO DISCOVER.'

One question emerges with unavoidable force: is there perhaps something more? Is there an area 'out of the box', or is there nothing? This question is more important than any other in life. And the later you face it, the more of life passes you by and you miss the real thing. If we face the nothingness, a silent invitation sounds in every moment: 'Stop with all the running away. There is so much more to discover.'

The problem is: you can only find this out on your own. Head knowledge or even a little educated faith is not enough. And with that, we come to the first exercise.

PRACTICE

OK, let's begin. There are three steps. The first step: find a place where, preferably, you will not be disturbed. You could also say: where there is nothing. The less there is, the better. Perhaps not the room you are in now, but in a room where there is no one else. A quiet park bench. A hidden part of the garden. A quiet clearing in the forest. A pew in a church. To do the exercise properly, it would be good to set aside as much time for this retreat as possible, at least to be able to stay in this place on your own for fifteen minutes. The next step is a little harder. It is: turning off. It works by actually turning something off. Your mobile, for example. And it should now stay off. Turn the music off. If others live in the house with you, then close the door. Try to put anything that distracts you into 'flight mode'.

A little harder is turning off the volume inside your head. It may only now become apparent how much there is going on there. Unfortunately, you can't mute your thoughts without going further. But one small decision can help. For these fifteen minutes everything is irrelevant. If there are any thought patterns or any 'to-dos' in your head that are so loud that they simply won't go away, then, before you start the fifteen minutes, take a pen and paper, and list each point, with an 'off button' next to each one.

Well, that was the hardest part. What happens now is very easy: open your hands. This small gesture might seem unimportant, but it says a lot. All day long we have our hands full with things to do. There is so much to carry. You can't simply put your hands in your lap – you have to take your life in both hands, hold it firmly, and take what you can get. The natural inner attitude of everyday life is one of closed hands. Now is the time to let go. Even of your mobile phone. Open out your hands. We brought nothing into the world and will take nothing away with us. No one really has life in their hands. Does it feel like a pointless game? It is more than that. Only those with open hands can receive a gift. Only those with open hands can rest. For today, it is enough to just try to sit for fifteen minutes with open hands. Don't worry: this small gesture is not nothing, it can make a real difference. God is here. He is the Creator, the one who has given you everything, who you are and what you have. And in the nothing – then everything

can be rich and full and deep. But this only comes to those who discover the foundation of life. And that is God. He is not hard to find, when the distractions are turned off and the hands are open. Do you understand? Try it!

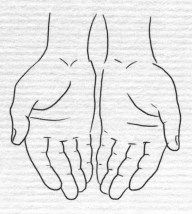

CHAPTER 2

THE SECRET

Safely hidden in the inside pocket of my torn denim jacket: the secret. No one can see it. It is written on lined pink paper and in surprisingly regular writing, in dark ink. Handwriting sloping slightly to the left, in fountain pen. How is it that girls write so tidily? The only thing missing would be for the letter to be scented. But it doesn't need to be scented for it to have an aroma.

The leaves fall from the trees on the way home from school; they are already golden brown. The words on the paper make everything different. It is not only the autumn afternoon that rests in a warm glow; somehow, everything seems bathed in a different light. In my Converse trainers, there's a bounce in my step. The scent of the warm evening. Things look different in the mirror when I'm at home later. Lost in thought, my hand brushes a strand of my long hair from my forehead. That she could watch me for hours. That she felt awkward when my eyes met hers. I can hardly believe it. Because, in the mirror, exactly the same face looks back at me as yesterday. The face about which I can't decide as to whether it looks stupid or cool. Behind the round glasses, brown eyes that just say nothing to me. Exactly those eyes that she is now writing about. Can it be true?

The letter is unfolded and read again literally dozens of times, just to be sure. Yes, it really is there. Only I know about it. It is my secret. The secret that I have been harbouring since this morning, like a treasure that no one knows about. And in the light of which, all at once, my world seems different. The treasure that changes everything: that there is someone who loves me. That's exactly what it says. And who calls me beautiful. Me, the somehow always-too-small teen, the rather skinny type with long curly hair and weird hipster clothes.

From now on it doesn't bother me so much whether the others find me cool or not. Because she is astonished by my eyes. It doesn't matter who likes my style, when she says I'm beautiful. The worries of next week also lose their heaviness. Even the upcoming maths test (I am so bad at maths). But even that blurs, because I am loved. And in my life there is suddenly a secret. A hidden treasure that makes me rich. The idea that love really does change everything, is suddenly a reality.

THE SECRET

Everyone has them, and everyone wants them. Shall I tell you a secret? Who wouldn't answer, 'Yes, go on!' It isn't only children who love to have a secret, or to be told a secret. Adults also have areas in their lives about which not everyone is allowed to know. That only close friends can be trusted with, or even no one. There is no life without secrets.

The problem is that not all of our secrets are praiseworthy. There are some things that, deep down, we are not proud of, or even that we are ashamed of. How would you feel if someone could browse through your computer, read your personal journals and watch you in your home? It is generally accepted that everyone has an

internal and an external persona. The external is what people can see with their eyes. What you know about a man. What colleagues and neighbours also know. The public self, and the side which we show to others.

And yet, there is also the inner self. That which is hidden from the human eye. Or that only those who know you well can guess. The riches behind the facade, the deeper level beyond the mask. This inner self is more important than the outer self.

Jesus put it like this: 'What good is it for someone to gain the whole world, yet forfeit their soul?' (Mark 8:36). Yet what is there in this inner place? Therein a secret is hidden, one that really can change everything. Are you ready?

Here comes the secret: you have a human spirit. Full stop. That's it. And now to explain: I don't mean a ghost or a fairy, but something that only humans have. Animals have an instinct and also a will. Yet in humans there is something that categorically differentiates us from animals and which can't be reduced to biology. Only humans can distinguish between good and evil. Whilst animals can think, only humans can designate something as true or false. And finally, only humans can make art, hang jewellery around their necks or write poetry. Philosophers hold these three special properties together: the Good, the True and the Beautiful. All mankind strives for these three goods; our lives would be terrible without them. Someone who has enough to eat and yet must do wrong, who lives in falsehood and without beauty, will not have a fulfilled and happy life. Yes, a life like that would actually be

subhuman. We are not just matter. We are literally 'out of the box', because nature and evolution alone can't explain why humankind searches after these things. He does it, because he's made in the image of God. God himself is the source of all goodness, all truth, all beauty. He is the fulfilment of all human searching.

The human spirit has the capacity to know God. To know God?! That is just unbelievable! The uncreated, eternal, limitless God? Yes, exactly! And because of this, the secret is so massive. And it gets even better! There is a place in you where you can meet this God. The image which I like best for this is that of an inner garden. In the biblical story of Creation, God puts mankind in a garden:

> *The LORD God took the man and put him in the Garden of Eden to work it and take care of it.*

GENESIS 2:15

The term 'garden' was not understood in biblical times to be the kind of mixed landscape of broccoli beds, box hedges and children's swings that we know today. A garden was a luxurious park for rich people, an extremely beautiful place. And what happened there? Very simple: God and man met each other. In a way, our own hearts are like a garden for meeting with God. The problem is that the story of Adam and Eve didn't go well. And in that state, without Jesus, this garden in us is pretty broken and dead. For this reason, not everyone who searches inside himself meets God. Anyone who searches honestly within knows that everything is far from OK. This 'not OK' is what the Bible calls sin. God is a God of love and truth. All in me that is not love and truth separates me from God. In humankind our natural place for meeting God has died. Paul describes it like this: 'And you were dead in the trespasses and sins in which you once walked,' (Ephesians 2:1 ESV).

GOD HIMSELF IS THE SOURCE OF ALL GOODNESS, ALL TRUTH, ALL BEAUTY.

Yet whoever invites Jesus to come into his heart and take away everything that separates us from God, whoever truly repents of whatever is sinful in his heart, and whoever believes in the power of the blood of Jesus to wash his sins away, in him something completely new happens. The miracle of salvation. The inner garden begins to bloom. It will be beautiful again.

And here is the deepest secret. That which Jesus has done on the cross, for every single one of us, works not only for when we go to heaven. His blood is pure and beautiful before God. That means God looks at you with a look of joy and wonder. He calls you beautiful! That is the secret. It is significantly more impressive than a pink letter that a teenager gets sent. Because this sender is decidedly more important. If you know you are loved, that changes everything. Life appears in a new light. It doesn't matter what people think. It doesn't matter what you look like. That is a secret that no one can take away.

Prayer is the way to understand that secret, to feel and to learn to live by it. And that changes everything.

PRACTICE

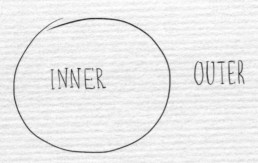

EXERCISE 1

This time it gets creative. You will need a pen and to draw a circle. First of all, it's about the difference between inside and outside. What areas of your life would you assign more to the outside? What are you busy with, which roles do you play, and what do people know about you – but which ultimately is only the outer self? You can write all that around the circle.

The circle itself stands for the inside. What makes you special? What does no one know about you? Where are you completely yourself? If you think of anything, you can write it in the middle. If you can't think of anything, it isn't a problem. It just shows that there is an exciting path of discovery ahead of you.

You may also realize that you don't fully know Jesus in the deepest parts of you, that not everything is OK there. You can tell him, in simple words, what's wrong, what you have done wrong. Then raise your inner gaze to the man on the cross. He did that for you, out of love. Do you believe this love? Then ask him to purify you with his blood and to come as Lord into the innermost part of your heart. If you have not been baptized yet, this would be the right time to contact the leader of a Christian community in your area. If you are already a Christian believer, may you trust that this beautiful garden already exists in you. Maybe it is a bit overgrown.

The inner garden is of course only an image. But pictures have power. With very simple strokes, you might imagine the garden like this. (In real life, of course, it is a lot more beautiful!):

EXERCISE 2

Now, it is recommended that you repeat the exercise from the first chapter (switch off and open your hands). It is a statement of our faith that man has a spirit, in which we can meet with God. The fact that the place of encounter is not somewhere in the hereafter, but in the heart of man, is one that many are unaware of. Take another fifteen minutes, and try to see if you can perceive this place inside. It is not about great feelings. It does not matter if at first you feel nothing. This little gesture of attentiveness and faith is enough to be sure that there is a place reserved for God in the depths of your heart. And that he loves to be there. And that he calls you beautiful, because Jesus has washed you clean and the garden has blossomed in you. God enjoys this time you give him. With this assurance, the second exercise ends.

CHAPTER 3

NOW

I'm so happy! Finally, a day at the sea once again, after such a long time. The train to Toledo doesn't leave until tomorrow. After the rainy days that have followed us all the way from the barren plateaus of Castile to the hills of Galicia, we're looking forward to a few hours of sunshine on our last day on the northwest tip of Spain. La Coruna is a vibrant harbour city. A little rundown in some places, yet full of life, with steaming plates of freshly caught lobster and all kinds of seafood on every corner of the narrow streets. For the first time, after a week in Spain, we breathe the salty sea air. Finally, a day at the beach, and finally, some sunshine.

A slightly worried look at the sky – will the weather change? We arrive at the beach and it is a bit windier than we had expected. We dig a small hollow in the sand and stretch out our towels – this works. Should we go in the water later? Actually the sea should be warm enough in August. It would be a shame to have brought all our swimming things with us for nothing.

The morning passes unhurriedly, and by noon, despite the wind, the sun shines down mercilessly. We hadn't thought of suncream! So off we go again to buy some suncream from a small shop for an outrageous price. Getting there and back again takes much longer than I had thought, and I make a hat by tying the corners of some clothing together. Suddenly, the thought strikes me: if we want to catch the train in the morning, we will have to be out of the guest house so early that maybe we should check out today. What if it takes too long to cross the city? I start planning and brooding. Then, I cast a look to the west – a front of blue-grey clouds is coming. Is that the end of the sunshine? If it begins to rain, it could get really cold. We work out how to pack our things together as quickly as possible. Once again we discuss tomorrow's departure. It's too late for swimming anyway. And added to that, we want to get some groceries.

We leave.

MISSED

Behind us is the glistening bay of La Coruna, the screech and scream of seagulls far above, cargo ships blur in the hazy distance and the spray slaps the rocks in the surf. Somehow I had not really noticed all that. But now it is too late. And I had been so looking forward to this day.

NOW

It only dawns on me much later: I have somehow missed our wonderful day at the sea. But how? Initially, I had been looking forward to it. Then I thought a lot about how the day would go. Then I waited. Then I took precautions. Then there was a lot to plan for the departure. And then finally, sitting in the small shabby guest house, the day by the sea was over, and the glittering light on the hot sand was extinguished.

The only moment that is really real, is now. Now is the moment when time and eternity meet. Of course, there is also the past and the future. Yet they are only important as they influence the now. God calls himself 'I AM' (Exodus 3:14) – he is the one who is fully present. And to be present means to be in the here and now. God is always in the here and now, you could say. The only problem is that we are usually not to be found there!

Don't you see? Look at yourself, in your life. What are you thinking about? Where are you, inside? Whenever you have a couple of minutes of quiet you will notice – you are somewhere else, dreaming of being somewhere else, either in the past or the future. You are already thinking about tomorrow, because there are so many worries awaiting you there. Or you hang on to yesterday, because you have screwed something up. You are sitting here, but in your mind you are already two stops away.

> **GOD IS ALWAYS IN THE HERE AND NOW. THE ONLY PROBLEM IS THAT WE ARE USUALLY NOT TO BE FOUND THERE!**

What a pity!

Because the sun, sea and seagulls are always only in the here and now.

Real life only takes place here and now. And God is always in the here and now. He is not hard to find. He is waiting for us. Only we are mostly somewhere else. It's high time we came back.

Jesus teaches total, carefree trust in the Father.

Therefore do not worry about tomorrow, for tomorrow will worry about itself. Each day has enough trouble of its own.

MATTHEW 6:34

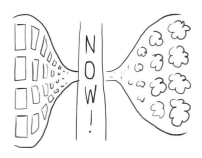

That is, however, easier said than done. It begins with learning to perceive that God is really real – really here. In the here and now. It actually sounds more mystical than it is. Immediately, the present moment is already gone. The immediate, the blink of an eye, is reality. To say that God is in the now, means only that he is real. That he is always waiting to meet with us. And therein lies our problem. The worrying, the thinking – our future life robs us of the joy of what is waiting directly before our eyes. Behind are fear and lack of trust. With one foot always in the next appointment, we are never quite present for what is taking place in the immediate moment. Nor for the presence of God, who can *be* in every second of life.

PRACTICE

You can grow into learning how to be in the here and now. Look once more for a quiet place and take around fifteen minutes to yourself. Close your eyes and try to simply be there. Perhaps you will notice at first how little you are 'here and now'. It doesn't matter. Many people don't notice this their whole lives long.

Once you have done this, step two is to imagine Jesus sitting

opposite you in the room. The idea is not so very strange, because Jesus is risen, and lives. Literally, he says:

> 'And surely I am with you always, to the very end of the age.'
>
> MATTHEW 28:20

That means here and now. You can talk with him like a good friend. You don't need to be torn away by yesterday and tomorrow, because you can talk to him about them. Give them to him. He can heal the past. And perhaps you would like to tell him about something that you have done wrong, and that you wish could have happened differently. Or, you want to bring him something which is troubling you, a conflict or something that is awaiting you tomorrow. It doesn't have to be very long, yet you will notice that there is a difference. If a problem is so big that it simply won't go away, you can do a worry-transfer contract with Jesus. He said:

> *'Come to me, all you who are weary and burdened, and I will give you rest.'*
>
> MATTHEW 11:28

If you want to, on a sheet of paper, write the worries that you have just given him.

This is just a first idea, a first step. The life in the present is far more all-encompassing. A very simple and much deeper secret. That God is here. That he is real. But for this, we must first be in our own present, not alone in the future or in the past. The present moment gives us the reality of God. He is the 'I AM'. Here and now.

CHAPTER 4

MINDFULNESS

Claire: Hi Ellen!

Ellen: Morning, Claire! How're things?

Claire: Oh, I don't know. I'm in a bit of a muddle really.

Ellen: Tell me about it. Same with me. My parents are coming to visit this weekend, the dog is at the vet and Monday is somehow never my day.

Claire: Well, actually for me, nothing much is new. But somehow I'm just feeling a bit flat.

Ellen: No wonder, with the stress of the last week! It was the same for me: all hell broke loose – first with the dog and then also the car breaking down.

Claire: Well, for me it wasn't that there was very much to do. I'm just starting to wonder whether this job is really what I want to do …

Ellen: Yes, I know what you mean. I just find it's all about my attitude, so I go for a run and then get in the shower, and I'm back on form straight away.

Claire: I've just come to realize that I started here right after my training and never really thought about what I should do with my life.

Ellen: Exactly! You need a new challenge. I love challenges. Like this new project at work. It's really innovative. I've loved being able to think of new ways of working, and I have changed the way the whole office runs. You should try something new too.

Claire: Hm. Yes, perhaps … I'm not sure right now what it is I need …

Ellen: How about a trip!? That always works for me, and then I come back refreshed and work doesn't seem so boring anymore. Travel is the solution. I always have my best ideas on holiday.

Claire: OK … well, last year I went to Majorca, and before that to Turkey …

Ellen: You can forget Majorca. It's become far too expensive. Last year I went island-hopping in the Aegean. Heavenly. The best was the view from the hotel in Rhodes. I must tell you about it – we drove for hours and took a ferry, and we were the only ones there who weren't Greek. Not one of them spoke English … And we tried to say hello, and then …

(…a long story and seventeen minutes later …)

Claire: But I don't actually want to go on a trip.

Ellen: Oh, of course. You're right – it's a check-up you need. It might be chronic fatigue. You should find out what's causing it. Whenever I'm too tired, it's iron deficiency – I simply have to go … (hours later …)

MINDFULNESS

Every relationship lives on it. And maybe you know conversations that have run like this. Claire certainly doesn't leave the conversation feeling that she has been understood. Why is this? Ellen has somehow listened and even given advice. But did you notice that she did not really grasp what Claire's issue really was? Many conversations are exactly like this – with people half listening and quickly interjecting, 'I know what you want to say.' Or not even that – it becomes just about wanting to tell your own story. Because real listening is not easy. It means becoming empty of one's own concerns. Giving the gift of time to the other person. Not thinking ahead as he or she shares. It also means being attentive, and asking thoughtfully targeted questions.

Often we are so full of our own thoughts that we skip over real listening. This is how we hold 'conversations' which are actually not conversations at all, but just a juxtaposition of monologues. You start telling me something, but I don't listen because I'm waiting for a pause so that I can tell you something of mine.

I have a very simple theory. And that is that prayer and loving have a lot in common. Because in order to love a person it means to be with them, to listen to them and to really hear them. When I give my full attention to what someone is saying, without immediately replying, that person feels accepted. Everyone longs for this, not to be immediately given advice or a lecture. 'Are you listening to me at all?' is more of a rhetorical question. Because

LEARNING TO PRAY IS LIKE LEARNING TO LOVE: IT'S EASY BUT IT COSTS YOU EVERYTHING.

What do you see on this page?

•

if you don't listen to me, you will not take in what I'm saying. You are not really hearing me.

Learning to listen and to hear is actually harder than one might think. Everyone who lives in relationship knows this is true. And at the same time it is the simplest thing in the world, just to give someone your full attention. Learning to pray is like learning to love: it's easy but it costs you everything. We are not all that good at really hearing. For example, what do you see in the picture on the previous page? One possible answer: a large white area. Or another answer: a black frame with six words in spidery handwriting. But more likely your answer will be 'one dot.' Unfortunately, I have to disappoint you. In the black box there are two dots (one smaller on the left side, half way between the big dot and the bottom edge). And if you also count the dots of the letters (because it's all about what you see on this page) there are four dots. Actually it is not even a black box, but four very inconsistent black lines that get thicker and thinner.

Did you notice that the lines don't meet top right or top left? And that there is a small tail bottom right? Of course, that was a bit of a mean trick. But it shows how often we only take in a part of something. In fact, our brain is made that way – it constantly fades out a large part of reality. What colour the sweater of the supermarket cashier was, and how many shelves of dog food I walked past. The brain has registered all of this. But I have not taken it in.

WE HAVE AN ANTENNA FOR THE PRESENCE OF GOD. BUT IT CAN BE WELL TUNED, OR POORLY TUNED.

What I am saying is, it is not difficult to perceive God. And to be exact, I'm not just talking about 'thinking' about God, but about really perceiving his presence. Because you can do that. Just because we can't see him or touch him, does not mean that he is not real. There are all kinds of things for which we humans have no physical sense. We can't perceive radioactivity, for example. But we also cannot perceive freedom, the relationship between two people, conflict or guilt. Nevertheless, we have antennae for all of these. Likewise, we have an antenna for the presence of God. But it can be well tuned, or poorly tuned.

The amazing thing about God is that he is always there. 'For in him we live and move and have our being', says the Apostle Paul (Acts 17:28). God does not live in another world that has nothing to do with ours, he is in the here and now. And what brings you back to the here and now is perception.

People of all religions and cultures perceive something of the divine. Only through Jesus, however, do we have direct access to the Father; we can personally meet and get to know God. And this is not difficult, but it requires breaking out of the circles of your own thought processes. And instead to have your eyes open, to be aware and mindful of him.

PRACTICE

EXERCISE 1

What comes next is the simplest thing in the world, and at the same time is the biggest challenge. The next two exercises are about learning to perceive. For the first one you need at least an hour of time and a little nature. The fields and meadows behind the village, a park in the city or a nearby forest. The less disturbed, the better. Find a nice little place where you can settle down undisturbed. There is so much to see in nature, it's unbelievable. And seeing is exactly what your one task is in this exercise. Take it all in. Allow yourself to perceive it. This usually starts with the eyes. Look around with the astonished eyes of a child at all that there is to see. The different shades of green in the leaves, the form of a branch, the shades of the sky. You can consider a whole landscape or even a single leaf. In either case there will be a lot to take in, to be mindful of, more than you really can consciously see in an hour.

But then there are the other senses. Which sounds penetrate your ear? What does it smell of? What does the wind in your hair feel like? And the pebbles under the soles of your shoes, or the bark on the tree? The important thing is to perceive – do not try to evaluate or analyze. It is not, for example, significant whether you know that it is a birch or lime tree standing in front of you. Or whether you like the road, or the weather. Just accept and allow yourself to perceive it. And do not rush from one to the next, but remain amazed by one thing, until you really have taken in the very depth of it. Please also do not try to interpret the impressions spiritually. Such as, 'Like this young branch, God also wants to bring my life to life.' Although such thoughts can be good and right, they go beyond pure perception. The purpose of the exercise, however, is to allow everything to be as it is, without imposing an interpretation on it. When you catch yourself thinking, just come back quickly to mindfulness. For this, it might help to ask the simple question: 'What is there?'

This simple look at nature goes deeper than you may realize. God has made everything. And when he had finished everything, he looked at it and found it to be 'very good' (Genesis 1:31). In just looking, you step into the loving gaze of the Creator, who wanted all that is there to be there. His creation has his favour. In his sight there is no stress; God rested on the seventh day. Concentrated watching can be exhausting. But that is not perceiving. That's why this exercise can be a great way to relax if you are stressed. But it is much more than that. Try it yourself!

PERCEIVE

EXERCISE 2

Perhaps you noticed in the first exercise how quickly you went from perceiving to thinking, to pondering and to exploring. Giving our full attention through mindfulness is even more important in contact with people, and this brings us back to the little story at the beginning of the chapter. The second exercise is that you consciously listen to someone. Only two kinds of answers are allowed – reflections, or queries to gain a better understanding. Reflection is expressing in your own words what you've heard to make sure you have really understood what the other person has said.

An example:

Claire: Hi

You: *Morning, Claire! How are you?*

Claire: *I don't really know. I'm just a bit confused ...*

You: *Confused?*

Claire: *Yes, totally. And I feel a bit flat.*

You: *So, you have no joy or excitement for life?*

Claire: *Absolutely not. I think it has to do with work.*

You: *Are you not enjoying your work?*

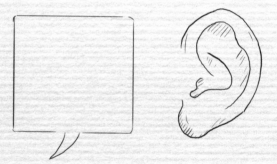

Do you recognize the difference in the conversation above? Here, someone really listens to, and really hears, another. This is reflected in the way that a piece of advice, or their own story, is not immediately given, but Claire's feelings are allowed to stand as they are. The exercise in nature was also not so much about the trees or thinking about the river. These things were just allowed to *be*. In real listening it's the same. You could even say that real love is like this. Paul once wrote in a famous chapter about love: 'Love ... rejoices with the truth.' (1 Corinthians 13:6). If you love someone, then you affirm them in their essence, as he or she is. That is easier in theory than in practice. Loving everything costs you everything. And it starts while listening. Be all ears. Really hear, really perceive what another is saying or feeling. If someone asks you something, you should of course answer, but your priority should be to let the other person have their say. To perceive another. This is the beginning of love. And the beginning of prayer.

CHAPTER 5

BODY

It isn't so very safe. Still, I only realize this as we turn and take a couple of steps into the narrow alley and curious, peering looks seem to follow us. I can't name the town, or the Asian country, because we are going to visit a Christian orphanage, one that was taken over by the state authorities. In this country Christians are always followed. There are mysterious arrests, intimidation, the threat of torture and brute force. We certainly feel safe, if only because we are Europeans. But no one knows we are Christians.

When, because of police surveillance, it becomes impossible for the local missionaries to approach the buildings, my wife Jutta and I decide to become one small undercover team. In our Western holiday clothes, and with rucksack and camera – just like tourists – we are perfectly camouflaged. Why shouldn't we happen to stroll through the streets, snap a couple of photos, as long as no one prevents us? Such naive thoughts!

Dirty rivulets at the side of the street where women wash clothes, scorching sun on palm leaves, rattling mopeds and the smell of the spicy street food. Barefoot children run after us. Curious glances from doorways. After only a few minutes it is clear that our action has not gone unnoticed. A foreign missionary who accompanies us dispels all doubt about the secrecy of our action.

'Forget it, Johannes!' he said. 'Everyone in the street knows you are missionaries.'

'Sorry?' I respond and look down at myself. I am not wearing a cross and nor am I carrying a Bible under my arm. And there are tourists in this city. How then would anyone recognize what kind of mission we are engaged in?

'Quite simply, the people here feel "a presence", your "aura".' I look dumbfounded. 'Aura?' I am not at all sure whether I believe in any such thing. And yet, whether or not I believe in it, the people here take it as truth. If anyone here becomes a Christian, he doesn't need any outer identification; the people around him feel it. Everyone notices, because something is really different. And when missionaries come to a remote village, people flock there. I have experienced it myself. Non-Christian neighbours crowd into the small room, so that we can lay hands on their sick children. Because they can feel that power is there.

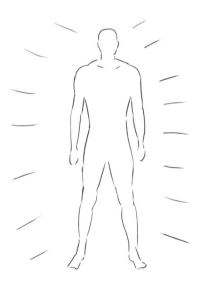

BODY

That there might be something more around my body, an aura – no, I don't believe in anything like that. And certainly not all that is made of it in the more esoteric circles. And yet, nevertheless, I can't deny that people throughout Asia and Africa clearly have experiences in the spiritual dimension, something that has to do with the physical body. With touch, or with presence. In the West, of course, we are not used to this way of thinking. Religion and faith are somehow 'head stories'. Inner attitudes and higher ideals. Not so very tangible. God simply has nothing to do with the material world, right? So should we renounce physical needs and pleasures, like the early monastics?

Indeed, it is only the Western world that sees almost nothing of the supernatural played out in the material. The body is just the physical body. If you are sick, you take pills. There is nothing spiritual about it. The biblical view of the human body is quite different. Even in Judaism it is ascribed a unique spiritual significance. And Jesus himself is no exception. He was no European, and did not share the Western, purely scientific view of the body. The Bible takes a holistic view. Man is a unity of mind, body and soul – inseparable. The body is therefore not merely a physical vehicle, but something essential. You are your body! While the Bible calls us not to be led by the flesh (see Romans 8:8–9), it is not referring to the physical body, but to the selfish tendencies of the heart.

On the other hand, we read something astonishing in Paul's letters.

Or do you not know that your body is a temple of the Holy Spirit within you, whom you have from God? You are not your own, for you were bought with a price. So glorify God in your body.

1 CORINTHIANS 6:19–20 ESV

The body is described as a temple. From this we can conclude several things. Firstly, the body is clearly important. In fact, the context of this biblical passage is a very tangible statement. The rest of the passage tells us: because your body is a temple of the Holy Spirit, you can't sleep with a prostitute. Bang. Yes, that's exactly what Paul writes. It's not just a statement about sex, but a completely different view of sexuality as a whole. It is a very concrete argument that outside the good plan of God, sexuality – the intimacy of man and woman – has a negative effect on the spiritual life. God created eroticism for one man and one woman in a close bond of love forever. Sex outside this playing field goes beyond the plan of God.

Yet Paul does not argue that one is forbidden and the other is allowed, simply because that is God's law. He lays the emphasis much more on the spiritual dimension of the body. Your body is a temple. You can't separate what you do with someone from the spiritual, even if you say 'it's only physical.'

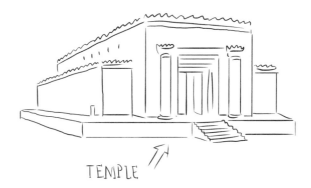

TEMPLE

There is more to this picture: in the Jewish understanding, the temple is the place where God lives and where you encounter him. The Jews went to the temple to pray, and that is exactly what Paul means in relation to the body. It is the place where the Holy Spirit lives. It's really remarkable that he doesn't write that it's the heart or the soul, where the Holy Spirit lives. No, it is the body!

This statement and the upcoming exercise may seem quite unfamiliar. But I suspect that may be because we have become accustomed to a way of thinking about the body, that has more to do with the philosophical tradition of the ancient Greeks than with the biblical, holistic view. Your body is a temple. It is not just a piece of flesh. When you belong to Jesus Christ, you become a temple of the Holy Spirit. And you can meet with God immediately there. But as for the here and now, it also applies to our bodies. Our bodies are always in the here and now, and we live in our bodies. But that does not mean we have learnt to perceive the Holy Spirit in the present. And so the next exercise should be of some help.

PRACTICE

KNEELING STOOL

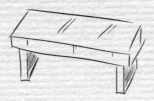

For this exercise you will need a kneeler or a stool, upon which you can kneel upright and in comfort. It's about finding a posture which can be held without effort, but in which you can't easily drift off or fall asleep. Find a position that you are able to hold, while remaining completely still, for twenty minutes. Then set a timer, or the stop watch on your mobile phone (not forgetting to put it in flight mode!).

I encourage you to do the exercise in three steps, either immediately one after the other, or over the next three days.

STEP ONE

In exactly the same way as you came to perceive nature in the last exercise, now you will begin to perceive your own body. Close your eyes and listen to yourself. It is not about trying to feel something in your own strength. Do not try to visualize your inner self. Just perceive what is there, if anything. It can help to go through the parts of your body one at a time. Allow yourself to sense each part. How are your feet on the ground? How do they feel? And your legs? Do you feel something from your lower back, from your spine?

Don't take it too fast, but let your attention – in wonder – rest on the individual areas of your body. It works better not so much as an exercise of forced concentration, but as one of loving listening. You may need to overcome some resistance, as this is more like meditation or gymnastics, but it just takes practice. Go slowly from your back to your shoulders, then the left hand and the left arm, then the right hand and the right arm. If twenty minutes is not enough time, it doesn't matter. Give it time. It's not about achieving something (that is never what prayer is about), but about an attitude of wholly being. Finish by focussing on your heartbeat. Do you realize that your own heart beats? God has made it and given you every heartbeat of your life. You can finish this short exercise by thanking him for it.

STEP TWO

We start again with sitting quietly. This time our attention rests only on our breathing. Breath is a mysterious thing. God himself breathed the breath of life into Adam (Genesis 2:7), Jesus breathed on his disciples (John 20:22) and the Holy Spirit is also described by the word 'wind' or 'breath'.

How do you perceive the flow of air through your body? Have you noticed that the air that you breathe in is cooler than the air that you breathe out? How does the air move up your nose? Follow it slowly, step by step, on its way through your head to the back of your throat. How does it flow, through the larynx and down into the bronchi? The air fills your lungs, your chest moves up and down. Can you perceive how it works, as your diaphragm lifts and lowers?

The Holy Spirit is the breath of life in you. Thank him for the gift of life!

STEP THREE

The first two stages were not explicitly about prayer, but were only preliminary exercises. In this third step, first briefly repeat steps one and two, and so centre yourself in your body and become aware of your breathing. Listen to yourself, and see if you can perceive the Holy Spirit living inside you. Again, you must only perceive, and not *do* anything. It doesn't matter whether you feel anything or not. True faith is not based on feeling something. But we can be attentive.

You can now say a few words to the Holy Spirit. 'Thank you that you dwell in me, Holy Spirit. Make me more aware of your presence.' 'Speak to me,' or 'Guide me.' Indeed, the power lies not in many words, but in listening for and feeling his presence. At first it may seem unfamiliar and even difficult. If it doesn't become clear to you, then go back and repeat the first two steps. I promise you: you can learn to be more attentive to the presence of God. At first while performing this exercise and then, more naturally, in your everyday life.

CHAPTER 6

DIMENSION

'Yes, I'm just coming!' While I clear the dinner table and put the plates in the dishwasher, Jutta puts our four children to bed. Our four lively, loud, funny and, mostly, very lovable children, who are calling for me now. Because naturally, Papa has to say goodnight. But then when I do, somehow, very little remains of the calm orderliness of the bedtime routine. Picture books are opened again, soft toys thrown around, the upper bunk is the scene of a wrestling match and someone has turned the CD player on again. So – lights out and everyone shooed to bed again. Everything is all just as normal in our family. But then again, not at all.

'Have you already prayed?' I ask.

'Yes, with Mama,' comes the response.

In our house, the children's prayer time is very practical. As we are in full-time service with the House of Prayer, we live by God's provision. Which means we live on what people give to us. We have made ourselves completely dependent on God, we don't receive any support from the state, church or employer. For our children, it means that we pray for anything that we need. Anything that we want. If we want to go on holiday, we pray that someone will give us a holiday. Which actually happens more often than not. Because God is faithful and truly acts on the prayer of faith, our children learn to pray without fear and very precisely. And to expect visions and impressions from God. And yet I am not prepared for what comes next.

Yes, they had already prayed. And our eldest son, Samuel adds: 'You know, Papa, I never used to know how to pray or how to ask God for something. Now I always go straight to heaven in front of his throne and receive what I need.'

Just a minute. Let me write that again. Here I am sitting between Playmobil and soft toys on the floor, and my eleven-year-old tells me that he 'goes to heaven'. And he goes into detail. In his mind's eye, he sees the throne room of God and he knows that we have access to this. That's why he goes there in spirit. And Anna (aged nine) adds, 'That's easy. I always explain this to people who ask what we live on. I say we do not have to worry because God supplies all our needs.' Right! I can hardly grasp this. I tell them another bedtime story (typically a Panda and a Giraffe are involved) and kiss them on the cheeks. As I go downstairs, I'm thinking to myself, 'This is exactly what true prayer looks like. Prayer that knows about … Dimension.'

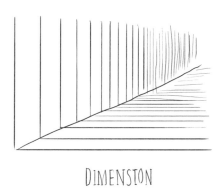

DIMENSION

DIMENSION

There are several of them in our world. One dimension is one level of reality. When something happens, it happens in more than one dimension at the same time. An apple falls from a tree. This movement happens in time and in three spatial dimensions. Physicists draw from this the existence of a number of other dimensions. But one thing is certain, the human senses are not always able to perceive all that really happens. In every era and culture people have believed in the existence of a spiritual reality. We know a whole lot about it. In fact, the Bible is full of stories of people who have been granted a glimpse of the heavenly dimension. But more than that, God himself became man so that we could have access to God and his kingdom. Many Christians think that the message of Jesus is only concerned with changing our behaviour, and to promise us eternal life. But he goes beyond that. He spoke of his kingdom, of a greater reality that had already begun in him, and will come to this world in abundance, when he returns in glory. But for now, one thing at a time.

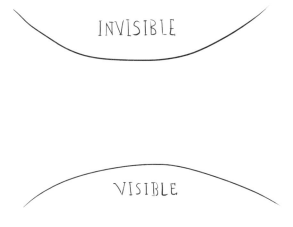

INVISIBLE

VISIBLE

Jesus spoke constantly of the kingdom of heaven as something that was coming, about to break in (Matthew 3:2). From a higher reality, one in which God rules. While much that happens on this earth is not in accordance with God's will, we wait for the day that only what is in the will of God happens and his kingdom breaks in. So Jesus taught us to pray:

> *'Your kingdom come,*
> *your will be done,*
> *on earth as it is in heaven.'*
>
> MATTHEW 6:10

But that is not all. Anyone who believes in Jesus, and through baptism and repentance is born again, will see the kingdom of God (John 3:3). Through Jesus we even have a place in this spiritual reality.

> *But because of his great love for us, God, who is rich in*
> *mercy, made us alive with Christ even when we were dead*
> *in transgressions – it is by grace you have been saved. And*
> *God raised us up with Christ and seated us with him in the*
> *heavenly realms in Christ Jesus.*
>
> EPHESIANS 2:4–6

It's important to note that this is not saying Jesus will give us a place in heaven, but that we already have access to it. Because of this the writer to the Hebrews can say:

> *Let us then approach God's throne of grace with confidence,*
> *so that we may receive mercy and find grace to help us in*
> *our time of need.*
>
> HEBREWS 4:16

We can and should come directly before God's throne. Or to put it differently, my son Samuel is right!

In the first five chapters of this book, the exercises were about meeting God in the real world, in the here and now. These steps

SITTING WITH CHRIST
IN HEAVENLY PLACES

are important, so that prayer doesn't become merely a matter of the head, but rather something anchored in reality; the spiritual belongs to this level of reality. In order to learn to perceive it better, inner pictures can help us.

One of the most important skills we have is the ability to imagine. Sportsmen and women know this – if a skier is to achieve a perfect performance in a downhill race, they must navigate the track countless times in their head beforehand. They have to visualize it. The things that are going on in our heads, whatever images are there, are of crucial significance. Perhaps God gave us the ability to imagine and visualize, so that we can gain access to spiritual things that our earthly eyes can't see. Because the spiritual reality is accessible to us only with a very special sensory organ: the eyes of faith. How did my son Samuel come across the idea to look with the eyes of faith?

Once a year, the MEHR conference takes place at our House of Prayer. Our children are enthusiastic participants in the parallel children's conference. This year our team of co-workers had the great idea of building the throne room of God, exactly as it appears in the Revelation of John. At first I smiled at the big, golden armchair on the stage, the floor of aluminium foil and the painted angels. And yet, in Samuel's changed prayer life it was clear to me: visual presentations have power, and influence the life of faith directly. In fact, the Bible gives us highly graphic pictures of the heavenly reality. Their meaning cannot be

THE SPIRITUAL REALITY IS ACCESSIBLE TO US ONLY WITH A VERY SPECIAL SENSORY ORGAN: THE EYES OF FAITH.

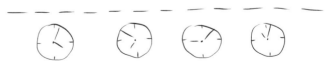

overestimated. It is all about what is eternal. Everything that we see on earth exists only for a certain time. Our own life lasts, at best, for a few decades, and buildings only last for centuries. But here we read of a reality that is forever.

After this I looked, and there before me was a door standing open in heaven. And the voice I had first heard speaking to me like a trumpet said, 'Come up here, and I will show you what must take place after this.' At once I was in the Spirit, and there before me was a throne in heaven with someone sitting on it. And the one who sat there had the appearance of jasper and ruby. A rainbow that shone like an emerald encircled the throne. Surrounding the throne were twenty-four other thrones, and seated on them were twenty-four elders. They were dressed in white and had crowns of gold on their heads. From the throne came flashes of lightning, rumblings and peals of thunder. In front of the throne, seven lamps were blazing. These are the seven spirits of God. Also in front of the throne there was what looked like a sea of glass, clear as crystal.

In the centre, round the throne, were four living creatures, and they were covered with eyes, in front and behind. The first living creature was like a lion, the second was like an ox, the third had a face like a man, the fourth was like a flying eagle. Each of the four living creatures had six wings and was covered with eyes all round, even under its wings. Day and night they never stop saying:

*'Holy, holy, holy
is the Lord God Almighty,
who was, and is, and is to come.'*

Whenever the living creatures give glory, honour and thanks to him who sits on the throne and who lives for ever and ever, the twenty-four elders fall down before him who

sits on the throne and worship him who lives for ever and
ever. They lay their crowns before the throne and say:

> *'You are worthy, our Lord and God,*
> *to receive glory and honour and*
> *power,*
> *for you created all things,*
> *and by your will they were created*
> *and have their being.'*

REVELATION 4:1–11

Some of these images may seem strange. But it is clear: the heavenly throne room is a very impressive place. And everything revolves around the centre point: God himself.

In the following exercise, we will use our imaginations. It is absolutely OK, and even helpful, to live one's entire life with the inner consciousness that this higher reality exists. That God is real and present. That he sits on the throne. That's why it is so bad when we fill up our visual memory with images that are negative. As what we let in through our eyes shapes our inside. Pornographic pictures are normal for many people today. Yet they are anything but harmless. Not only does the power of pornography make you dependent and destructive, it fills your imagination up with images of spurious abusive acts. The same applies to violence and horror movies as well as the majority of video games. Once something is stored in the brain, it usually stays there for a very long time, especially when it comes to visual data.

This is not about demonizing the media. But the imagination has great power. And the best thing you can do with it is to use it to give your heart a firm anchor in God.

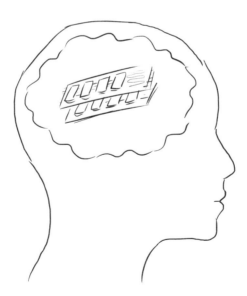

PRACTICE

In this exercise, you can fully develop your visual imagination. Live out your mood. Here is a sketch of the Old Testament temple.

In the past, when an Israelite wanted to pray, he had to go through various stations. There were different areas in the temple. Many were just for the priests, and one accessible only to the high priest. Since Jesus died and established the new covenant, there has been no more need for animal sacrifice; instead his blood washes us from our sin, and we each have direct spiritual access to the presence of God. The featured stations of the temple can help us to come to the Father with everything that matters to us. And this is how the exercise works: I describe one station, and then you close your eyes and imagine it and how you pray there. And then onto the next. You decide the pace.[2]

2 The idea of praying like this came to me as a teenager when listening to a talk by David Yonggi-Cho from South Korea.

FORECOURT

Those who wanted to enter the temple first came into an outer court and then an inner atrium. The way led from the external to the internal. In the forecourt, you would leave the everyday sphere and enter the sacred: the room reserved for God.

ALTAR

On a raised platform in the forecourt of the priests, there stood a large altar made of bronze. Through the offerings presented there, the people of the Old Testament would be cleansed of their sins. This was just a foreshadowing, pointing ahead to the one and only true sacrifice. When Jesus died on the cross, he washed us clean of our sins. God lives in inaccessible light. In their own strength, sinful mortals cannot stand before him. We can only come into

God's presence because Jesus' blood enables us. Imagine a cross on the altar and look at it. You can take a few minutes here to think about what Jesus did for you and thank him. The wonder of the miracle of salvation should never be lost on us.

BRONZE BASIN

Before the priests could perform their service in the sanctuary, they had to wash in a large water basin. On the surface of the water you would see your own reflection. As you reflect through this exercise, now is the moment to ask God to take away the things that separate you from him. These can be the sins that still burden you, or also just worries and stresses. Never hesitate to ask God to cleanse you. There is no perfect person. And God has no problem with that, when we come to him with all our weakness. But make it specific.

SEVEN-ARMED LAMPSTAND

You enter an actual sanctuary, a high gold-clad building. Inside this ornately carved room burn seven oil lamps on a large golden lampstand. This symbolizes the Holy Spirit. The Holy Spirit is our helper in prayer and the light for our eyes. Be aware of his presence (perhaps with the help of the breathing exercise in chapter 5), thank him for it and ask him to guide you in prayer.

SHOWBREAD

In the sanctuary there is a special table with loaves laid on it. A possible explanation is that it's a reminder of God's care for the people of Israel in the desert. Jesus emphasized that man does not live by bread alone, but from every word that comes from the mouth of God (Matthew 4:4). He called himself the bread of life

(John 6:35). At this point in your reflection, you could ask God for a word for the day. Listen to your inner self – can you perhaps imagine what God wants to tell you today? Another idea, at this point, is to read a short passage from the New Testament, or from the Psalms.

ALTAR OF INCENSE

The entire interior of the sanctuary is filled with incense, because the incense altar burned day and night. This is a symbol of the praise of God, by those who never fall silent before his heavenly throne. Now is the time for praise. You can do that in your own words: praise God for who he is. 'God you are faithful!'

Alternatively, you can sing, of course. Worship has a massive impact because it focuses our attention away from our problems and towards God. If you run out of words for what God is like, you will find many ideas in the Psalms.

HOLY OF HOLIES

A heavy curtain separates off a small chamber at the rear end of the building: the sanctuary, the Holy of Holies. In this mysterious, dark room stood the golden Ark of the Covenant. Under the old covenant, the glorious presence of God was made manifest here. Just once a year the high priest was allowed to enter this place. When Jesus died on the cross, the curtain was torn in two and since then, the way into the Holy of Holies has been made open;

anyone who believes in the Lord Jesus is free to enter. There is a deep silence in this mysterious room. Just stand in the presence of God and enjoy his presence and his love. You can decide for yourself how long you want to extend your time in the temple and when you have to return to your everyday life.

CHAPTER 7

SIGHT

I am not exactly the star of the class just now. Not one of the football team, nor cool enough to have a scooter. Rather, I am the skinny one who is good at Latin. And every morning I hold my breath for a moment as I set foot in the classroom. How will the others react to my outfit?

Because I always think I'm wearing something normal, a baggy sweater with red writing on it, teamed with a pair of jeans, for example. 'Hi,' I mumble, and walk over to my seat. At once there are mocking glances from all sides. The two girls by the window wrinkle their noses. 'What do you look like today?' asks my neighbour. And yet most of my classmates say nothing, they just look. What's wrong? The thought shoots through my head, as I look down at myself – what's funny about me? Is it my new experimental gel hairstyle, or the old sweater? It suddenly becomes my goal to look as inconspicuous as possible the next morning. Anything to avoid these goofy comments and strange looks.

The subject of appearance preoccupies me for a long time. What looks awkward, and what is cool? What looks do I get when I do something outstanding? If I keep in good contact with the school and its representatives, the teacher nods at me appreciatively. And yet from the far left corner of the classroom, eyebrows are raised in contempt and someone hisses that I am 'such a nerd.' The boys find me witty – do the girls think I'm silly? No matter what you do, someone always thinks it stupid.

Later I start to play around with this, and I consciously start to wear the craziest and most peculiar clothes. Why not a yellow checked shirt and green trousers, and that far too large T-shirt? And why not an Indian headband over my long hair, and, naturally, bright pink laces in my turquoise sneakers? For my friend and me, in a mix of punk and hippie, our aim is to draw as many strange looks as possible. It works quite well when I wear a Spanish sombrero. There is no chance of my blending in with the crowd; one would remember my completely crazy outfits. With curly locks, brightly coloured lounge pants, two jackets one on top of another, and chains around my neck, I felt great. Well, it was the era of the Kelly Family and Kurt Cobain; it was the nineties, after all!

Today I am glad that there aren't more photos of me from that time. Back then, though, I felt completely free, because I had settled it within myself that the looks of others were irrelevant to me. The teachers could think what they wanted. My classmates could whisper. I was only being myself, who I wanted to be. But that was, sadly, not completely true. I realized this at one point: I stood in front of an overflowing wardrobe, feeling clueless. What should I put on? Of course women have this problem quite often. I rummaged through my clothes, putting each item back again. Maybe this shirt? No, that was not crazy enough. But … I thought I was spontaneous, and didn't care what things looked like? Then it dawned on me – not only did I rather like the attention, but I was playing exactly the same game, just with a different set of rules. I did not want to stand out by adopting a fashionable look (Levi's 501s and Benetton sweatshirt) so now it was about acting as contrary as possible. It was my goal to draw offended looks. But I was still trapped by the same self-consciousness.

IN WHOSE SIGHT?

SIGHT

This seems to be an important concern for Jesus as well. And one that he puts right at the beginning of his first public sermon, as he starts to speak on prayer. It is Jesus' first major address, and the first thing he says on the subject of prayer – what could it be? To my astonishment, I discover that Jesus talks about how we should pray. Now, most believers think that one can pray anywhere. The question of where is unimportant, surely? But for Jesus it seems to be a little different. He says:

> 'And when you pray, do not be like the hypocrites, for they
> love to pray standing in the synagogues and on the street
> corners to be seen by others. Truly I tell you, they have
> received their reward in full. But when you pray, go into
> your room, close the door and pray to your Father, who is
> unseen. Then your Father, who sees what is done I secret,
> will reward you.'

MATTHEW 6:5–6

The point of this passage is not that one place is better to pray in than another. The question Jesus is asking, is: Who is watching you? Whose eyes are on you? Under whose gaze are you standing?

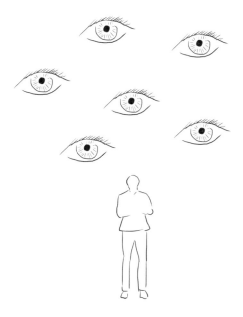

The question of whose gaze you are standing under is a deep question of the heart. And one that starts early on in life. Babies react to the gaze of their mother, even before they can speak. They *feel* whether or not someone sees them and whether they are seen. The research into how a small child looks at their primary caregiver is conclusive and impressive, showing the effect on learning and behaviour, and how the brain develops special mirror neurons that help the infant to understand the feelings of others and to start to enter into relationships. For a child, their own sense of being seen and perceived is vital. So a baby feels the gaze of their mother and father. In the course of their life this is added to. The looks of siblings, carers, teachers and friends. Finally, the aforementioned looks of the classmates and work colleagues.

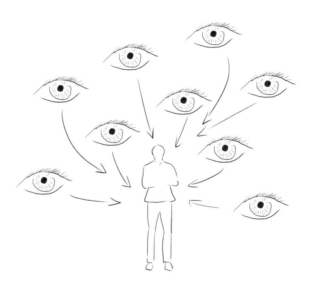

And very early on, children also learn that there are friendly, negative and disinterested looks. Everyone subconsciously gets used to behaving so as to elicit as little rejection and as much friendly attention as possible. The problem is that there are conflicting expectations connected with all of these looks. The teacher wants me to pay attention, but I get respect from my classmates when I'm the class clown. Many people can literally feel the expectations of others. The feeling of being watched and judged in the eyes of others can actually convey a permanent pressure of expectation. And often, you can feel these looks even when the people themselves are not there, maybe when they're not even alive anymore. There are more than a few who are still trying to earn affirmation in the eyes of their father, even though he may be long dead.

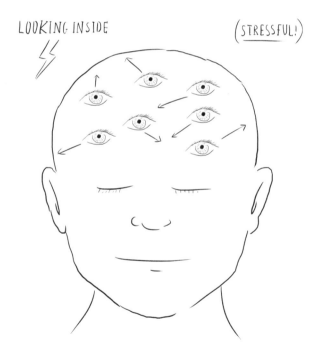

LOOKING INSIDE

(STRESSFUL!)

It is a lifestyle like that is far from free, in the deepest sense. And yet it is incredibly common and appears in different ways:

- comparing oneself with others
- feeling inferior to others
- feeling better than others
- needing to be better than the rest
- constantly looking in the mirror
- the conviction that one is always doing something wrong and never being able to do anything right
- the constant need to try to please everyone
- being in fear of man, so that you don't do what you want to.

These are all different expressions of an underlying attitude to life. It is the attitude of living life under the eyes of others. In the biblical story of Adam and Eve, we read that this problem with the eyes of others started pretty much as soon as their relationship with God was broken.

> *Then the eyes of both of them were opened, and they realised that they were naked; so they sewed fig leaves together and made coverings for themselves.*

GENESIS 3:7

It is a strange idea, that Adam and Eve hadn't noticed before that they had no clothes – that 'they knew that they were naked' goes deeper: all at once they could not bear to be just as they were. They started to hide, to dress up. And soon afterwards, Adam started to push the guilt of the whole disaster onto Eve. Eve, in turn, accused the serpent, and since then the mutual accusation that has run throughout human history has not stopped. Jesus taught and lived a radically different model. It was never his aim to appear good in the eyes of men. He said, 'I do not receive glory from people.' (John 5:41 ESV), meaning that praise and recognition in the eyes of men were not his motivation. Paul is no different:

For am I now seeking the approval of man, or of God? Or am I trying to please man? If I were still trying to please man, I would not be a servant of Christ.

GALATIANS 1:10 ESV

What a radical statement! It is not his aim to be praised by men! Like Paul, Jesus receives his power, his position and his authority not from men, but from God. But how can you learn to live like this?

There is a decisive moment in the life of Jesus. When he lets John baptize him in the desert, the heavens open above him.

LIKE PAUL, JESUS RECEIVES HIS POWER, HIS POSITION AND HIS AUTHORITY NOT FROM MEN, BUT FROM GOD.

One voice is heard: 'You are my beloved Son; with you I am well pleased.' (Mark 1:11 ESV). Jesus feels the pleasure of the Father. And after that he lives only in his sight. We can practise this way of life as well. And Jesus alone shows us the way.

But when you pray, go into your room, close the door and pray to your Father, who is unseen. Then your Father, who sees what is done in secret, will reward you.

MATTHEW 6:6

He speaks of a reward, of that which the Father gives to us. The reference point is the attitude of the hypocrites who get their reward through being seen by people. But what reward awaits those who seek God in secret? They will feel the loving gaze of the Father, and will gain a deeply liberated way of life, without pressure and full of power. This is life in the presence of God.

It is an absolutely revolutionary, simple fact: God is present. He sees you. And that doesn't just apply in prayer time, but in every moment of the day. When we understand this, everyday life is no longer mindless and no job in the world is blind drudgery. What would your workday look like if you were conscious in every moment that God sees you? And that loving look is your Father's reward to you?

You can stop comparing yourself to others, lusting after recognition from others, putting yourself under pressure and allowing it to control you. This life is the vocation of every Christian. But it starts with a specific time of the day, in which it is practised. This time is called prayer.

GOD IS PRESENT ... WHEN WE UNDERSTAND THIS, EVERYDAY LIFE IS NO LONGER MINDLESS AND NO JOB IN THE WORLD IS BLIND DRUDGERY.

PRACTICE

EXCERSISE 1

Maybe you have noticed that certain eyes always seem to be on you, even when you are alone. For the exercise today it is important that you look for a place where nobody can see you. Close your eyes and try to feel the inner looks that exist in your life. Who are you trying to please? Whose standards and expectations are on your shoulders? Whose approval is important to you? Can you assign these 'looks' to a person? Then pick up a pencil and draw a picture, like the one a few pages ago with the eyes inside the head. You can either label the eyes with a person's name, or with the role they play in your life. They can be very different. Some people have written the following when doing this:

- The inner impulse: A look in you that leads to seeking more and more power, that drives you, and makes you feel you are never good enough or fast enough.
- The inner prosecutor: A scornful look that shames you and passes sentence on you.
- The inner analyst: A look that means everything that you do is observed, commented on, dissected and checked in the minutest detail.
- The inner meanie: A look that tells you that you are bad and without value.
- The inner cynic/scoffer: A sarcastic view, which does not accept anything and takes nothing seriously.

Of course, these are not real people. But in the lives of many people, such inner perspectives and evaluators are amazingly firmly established. The key thing is: none of these views come from God. He is not the impostor, not the accuser, not the icy analyst. He is the Father who sees in secret and rewards you. Our loving, present Father who encourages and teaches his child. And nothing escapes

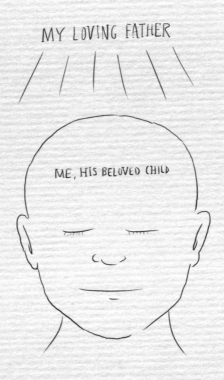

MY LOVING FATHER

ME, HIS BELOVED CHILD

his attention, he even rewards that which is overlooked by others.

This exercise is quite simple, it is to internally step out from the eyes of others, and stand under the gaze of the Father. This works best again with a picture. Imagine the scene: you are standing in a group of people, the eyes of the others resting on you. Maybe you can assign the different kinds of looks to individual people. And maybe you even feel the expectations and opinions of these people and the control they exert over your life now. But hold on now – remember you do not have to live like this. You can choose to live a life in the sight of God. Imagine yourself stepping out of the twilight of all these other looks and stepping into the bright light of God's gaze. Can you feel how this look of acceptance and love rests on you? If not, repeat that act of stepping several times. Out of the dark, into the warm beam of a bright spotlight. In this view, there is nothing special to do. Just like when the sun shines on the beach, so the only thing that changes under the gaze of God is time. Buds are coming into bloom under the rays of the warm spring sunshine. And the human heart is healed and whole under the loving eyes of the Father. When you have come into his sight, you can stay as long as you like. But don't leave this place too fast. This is the place of freedom. The place where you can be yourself.

CHAPTER 8

SURRENDER

Antipasto misto and a dry white wine. Two extra chairs have to be brought because the small restaurant is already overflowing. When Italians call for something, it always sounds as though they are scolding the waiter. Men in tight-fitting suits greet ladies of a certain age, who wear large hats with natural grace. And more and more people arrive.

'This is Professor Hellman,' whisper a group of new undergraduates, here near the university of Munich. I am invited to the inaugural lecture of a young professor of natural sciences – not my faculty – and to the celebration afterwards. I suddenly find myself in the middle of a cheerful group of celebrating luminaries. We have all gathered and ranks and names are given. Here professor so-and-so, there a rector and over there a director of a research institute. At first glance I don't notice him. A slender figure of medium height, in a fashionable grey suit, his nickel-plated glasses emphasising his fine facial features. 'That,' someone whispered to me, 'is him.' Surrounded by interested listeners, hanging on his every word. And *that* is his doctoral supervisor, the proposer of the young professor who is to be installed today. Not only that, but the founder and long-time director of the institute, bearer of numerous national and international awards, world famous researcher and undisputed master of his discipline. Respectful looks all round.

The main course is served. With loud Italian shouts, the sweating waiters push between the guests, steaming plates piled high with *saltimbocca*. Carafes of Chianti bring an even happier mood. Jackets already cast off and ties loosened, the luminary and the young professor finally sit down at our table. Congratulatory toasts from the venerable aristocracy of science. And easy conversation. Finally, the older, respected researcher says a few words. How happy he is that his young student took his suggestions so seriously, and this led – as he predicted – to a successful conclusion, that the support of a doctoral supervisor is the most important thing in a scientific career and that the results of the young scholar's research should be allowed to be counted as a component of the professor's own theories.

The professor draws his young friend, who is a little alienated by the emphasis on the merits of his doctoral supervisor, into the now clearly red-wine-fuelled conversation. It is clear that the elder is the better and more famous researcher. No question. But in tennis the old professor was usually defeated by the younger (amused laughter and approving nods from all sides). Suddenly, the old professor adopts a distinctly frosty expression. Emphatic contradiction follows. It had been decidedly different. He had only lost a single game at the institute trip last summer. Otherwise he had always won, sometimes even with a clear lead. The boy takes it lightly. Well, whether it really was that way, should be left open. But now, red-faced and clearly disgruntled, the old professor insists that it would be simply outrageous and in every way presumptuous to claim that he had lost in tennis. After all, he trains frequently and with the greatest vigour.

Embarrassed, the other diners try to change the subject as quickly as possible. And even before the profiteroles and the espresso are served, good humour is restored, one individual saying how he could not have been happier at the celebration of the newly appointed professor. Meanwhile, with a sour expression and looking askance, the founder of the faculty, the long-time director of the institute, winner of countless awards, internationally respected scientist, sips on his glass of grappa.

This rather amusing story actually happened, exactly like this. And it left me pretty bewildered. Only when I was sitting on the tube home, could I find words for what had actually irritated me so much. He was unequivocally the most famous academic to be invited to the celebration. And he had come to the conclusion he had to contribute something to this celebration – he was certainly the teacher and sponsor of the young researcher. But strictly speaking this evening was not about him.

It was a party for someone else. His behaviour seemed peculiar when he was so anxious to draw out his own importance. It became most ridiculous when it came to tennis. Was it really so unbearable for this important man that he was not as good at sport as the much younger scholar? This conduct, yes, the whole attitude of this great academic seemed completely self-absorbed. All his thinking and speaking seemed to revolve around himself.

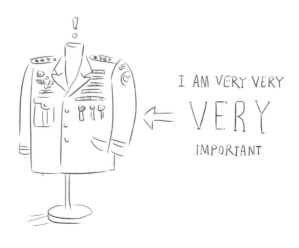

SURRENDER

Something has to yield, there has to be surrender, if we want to learn to pray. Self-centredness. The story of this crass, bizarre, grotesque scene actually describes a tendency from which none of us are immune. How many of our thoughts revolve around ourselves? How did I do at work today? What do others think of me? What plans and dreams should I pursue? How will I get justice, what I need or even just want right now? It's sobering to observe how much in our heart is actually just centred around ourselves.

In the normal course of everyday life, this is less noticeable. It is more obvious in relationships, in conversations like that between

Ellen and Claire described in chapter 4, for example. Who doesn't know an Ellen, who seems to always be talking about herself? Which of us, when quiet for just a few minutes – and yes, even when trying to pray – doesn't find ourselves faced relentlessly by this same tendency? Man revolves around himself.

Here are a few examples of prayer times when we might actually want to stand in the sight of God, or we might try to perceive the here and now, but we are in fact only preoccupied with ourselves:

- I think about my goals and plans. Maybe I even pray that God will bless them. But ultimately this is about my intentions and my will.
- Feelings of self-pity come over me. I mean, it's like life is passing me by. Everyone else is doing better than I am. My life is one big FAIL. And in thinking about all that I don't achieve, I am thinking only about myself.
- Suddenly, self-accusation is added to the mix. That prayer does not seem to work. I'm getting impatient with myself because everything seems to revolve around me, around what I'm doing right or wrong.
- Daydreams and musings ambush me, on a lonely island or in the past, where everything is beautiful. But actually I'm avoiding the presence of God that hangs firmly in the here and now – my reverie.
- It's hard to rest – because immediately thoughts flood in, of things I still have to do, weighing heavily on me. All that is waiting for me. All that I have to do seems to take on unimaginable importance. Ultimately, it all depends on me.
- I am dissatisfied with my prayer time. Shouldn't everything happen more quickly? And I can hardly concentrate. It has achieved nothing. And it did not help me so it doesn't make any sense.

This self-centredness is encountered by everyone who begins to pray. And this is exactly where the change begins, because self-centredness is the great enemy of love. Prayer, on the other hand, is the great leaving behind of self-centredness. That's why it's the great school of love.

SELF-CENTREDNESS IS THE ENEMY OF LOVE. PRAYER, ON THE OTHER HAND, IS THE GREAT LEAVING BEHIND OF SELF-CENTREDNESS.

PRACTICE
EXERCISE 1

Simply recognizing how self-centred our life is, that is the beginning of healing. Jesus did not come to treat the healthy, but the sick (Matthew 9:12). And those who know they have a problem are far closer to that healing. Just to come back, in prayer, under the loving gaze of God, after realizing that one's life revolves only around oneself, is a healing lesson in humility. It is not about perfection in prayer, but about giving oneself. But this means it's not up to me to rate the quality of my prayer. Am I dissatisfied with the 'result' at the end of my prayer time? That too is a sign of my self-centeredness. And that's why it's in the first exercise in chapter 1, and should be at the end of each prayer time: give the time back to the Lord and let him judge it. You can end with a very simple prayer that goes something like, 'Lord, today I have felt nothing, and it has felt as if praying has been pointless. I give this time to you now and do not want to evaluate it. I did it out of love for you and not for me. Thank you for taking this time in your hands.' Whether there were any great feelings or nothing at all: it's not about me, it's about him.

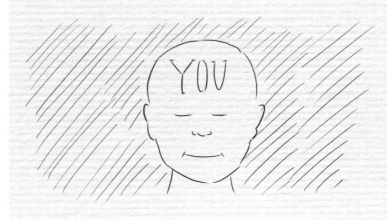

EXERCISE 2

This second exercise, one that is directed firmly against our self-centeredness, comes from Jesus himself. When asked how we should pray, Jesus answers with the Lord's Prayer. Everything in this prayer is a departure away from the self and a turning towards him. The exercise today involves slowing down the Lord's Prayer, section by section, to pray and to do it inwardly. First, read the instructions, then you can start.

YOU ARE
MY
FATHER

OUR FATHER IN HEAVEN

The prayer begins with turning our eyes to the Father. The perception of his presence. The heavenly reality that I can meet with him in the here and now. Right from the start, there is a turning from 'I' to 'You'. It's all about him, the Father in heaven, the one to whom Jesus has opened the door for us.

HOLY IS YOUR NAME

The first petition, and the first request of the prayer is: 'Your name should be made big! You should stand tall, you should be Number One in my life, and in the whole world.' When speaking of things that go beyond everything else, we say, 'That is sacred to me.' He himself is the highest goal and that is what this is actually all about.

IT'S ABOUT HIM

YOUR KINGDOM, YOUR HONOUR

YOUR KINGDOM COME

You shall rule! Before I talk about anything, please, it must be made clear that God should be the Lord of everything.

THY WILL BE DONE, ON EARTH AS IT IS IN HEAVEN

Your will also happens in my life. This plea is a real surrender. We can only do this safely because we know that God is a loving Father. Therefore, his will is always perfect and infinitely better than anything we could plan or desire for ourselves.

YOUR WILL NOT MINE

AS IN HEAVEN

SO ON EARTH

GIVE US TODAY OUR DAILY BREAD

You know what I need. I trust that you will supply my needs. Maybe not in advance for the next twenty years. But day by day. And maybe not with everything I dream of, but with all that I really need, every day. Therefore, I can ask with confidence.

AND FORGIVE US OUR SINS

Many people think themselves to be pretty good, if they are honest. It goes like this: 'I have not killed anyone and I'm no different to anyone else, therefore I'm not such a big sinner.' The biblical view of man is more realistic. Everyone has areas in their lives that are not OK. The problem is that we have blind spots. When we pray this prayer, we are letting go of these patterns of self-justification. We leave it up to God to judge us, and humbly acknowledge that we need mercy.

FORGIVENESS

AS WE FORGIVE OUR DEBTORS

Our refusal to forgive others shows how self-centred we are. But only those who forgive others emerge from that endless cycle of self-pity and accusation. Forgiving others does not mean denying wrong has been done. It is a simple recognition that we ourselves are not without mistakes and therefore we concede the same for others. And it is a decision not to hold on to reproach or bitterness.

AND DO NOT LEAD US INTO TEMPTATION, BUT DELIVER US FROM EVIL

The point of this request is not that it is God's intention to test us. It is the humble confession that one might be seduced. Each one of us is capable of far more evil than we realize. On our own, we are not very resistant or good at liberating ourselves from evil entanglements. God is our Great Redeemer. He can save us from temptation, from bad habits and dangerous situations.

Pray the Lord's Prayer in the awareness of these truths. After that only one thing remains: the reminder that it is not perfection that matters. How well this exercise has worked is not important. What is important is that you decided to look at him and not at yourself. The more often personal prayer time happens, the bigger the impact on your whole life. If something really has changed, hopefully your fellow human beings will notice. They will notice, for example, when you are really listening and not full of your own thoughts.

CHAPTER 9

TRAFFIC

No, that is not fog, that is smoke. And no, it is not the weather, but someone's idea to burn rubbish somewhere. Or perhaps a couple of hundred thousand too many motor-rickshaws in too small a place (without exhausts, you understand). My first close encounter with the traffic in Mumbai will not fade fast from my memory. OK, the traffic in Cairo, Bangkok or Chicago is also something to be reckoned with, yet everywhere else in the world I find there is a certain something missing, an extra level of insanity that, in this Indian chaos, adds a few extra degrees of spice to the curry. Everywhere and in every corner there is the poverty, the misery and the dirt in which people have to conduct their daily lives.

And essentially, of course, why have a traffic light, if you can have a horn? It is possible to survive the Indian traffic in any conceivable vehicle as long as it has a horn. A truck overturned at right angles to the road? A sacred cow trotting calmly about the road? Or just a bend in the road? You can always honk your horn – for virtually any reason, or for the lack thereof.

The three women sit behind, squashed into the narrow back seat of the tiny rickshaw. I squeeze myself to the left of the driver, preoccupied with holding on tightly with both hands so as not to be thrown off as this tin box rattles around the bends. Down a dirty side street and through an underpass at a foolhardy pace. Honking straight into a crowd of other equally honking rickshaws. Like a pack of hunting dogs, a whole bunch of noisy yellow minicabs shoot towards the wide main road, with colourfully embroidered veils and the limbs of passengers dangling out, front and back. In order to get across the intersection, it's best not to think at all. There are donkey carts, bicycles, cows and vans on all sides. From colourful, hand-painted trucks, to stoical drivers mounted on carts, to small Japanese cars, it is all far too much. A single horn screams through the south Indian dust, dirt and heat. Every vehicle seems to be going exactly in that direction, where a whole convoy of other vehicles is completely blocking the way.

How we got across this intersection in our rickshaw is, in hindsight, not entirely clear. But the bearded driver next to me spits a stream of orange betel nut spittle into the street beside us, honks several times and then just drives into the middle of the confusion. Somehow we thread and wind our way through. As if the chaos was not already total, I now see, in the middle of the intersection, a policeman, baton in his hand and beige pith helmet on his head, busy trying to direct the traffic. He blows his whistle incessantly, but the impact of this measure is unclear to me. Then, all movement stops. With loud shouts, street vendors push between the vehicles, offering nuts and self-adhesive sun visors for cars (why, of all places, on this intersection?). A sudden acceleration pushes me back into the seat and I have to tighten my grip on the struts of the small vehicle to avoid falling out. A tiny gap in the traffic has opened up in front of us, and this has to be taken advantage of quickly. Now, in front of us and to the left, a temple appears. The small pink building consecrated to the elephant-headed god, Ganesha, is decorated with red and green plastic garlands. Deafening music in honour of the god rattles and roars from loudspeakers, and over this is the penetrating crooning of a woman's voice.

'How do you like India, sir?' With a toothless grin, the turbaned driver turns first to me, and then to the back. 'Whoa!' I think, 'Watch the traffic!' I manage to stutter, 'It's lovely, it really is.' When he finally stops in front of our hotel, I find a crumpled rupee banknote from my bag and climb out. Once again grateful to still be alive. Looking forward to a few hours of relaxation that await us in this quiet hotel on the outskirts of the city. Shower first. Air conditioning. Finally, silence. Outside the window, green hills spread out far below: the foothills of the city with its countless corrugated iron settlements. A cup of tea. It is still a few hours until the lecture tonight. Hours when I want to spend time with God and prepare myself. Here, there is nobody to disturb me. So I kneel, close my eyes, and start to pray. A few deep and relieved breaths.

IN MY
HEART =
MUMBAI

But then suddenly: a horn sounds. The vibration of the traffic below. The noise of the street, the smell of sweet patchouli rising from swathes of incense sticks, the distorted bass of speakers turned too high. Mumbai is back. In graphic detail too. The faces of the women with their heavy water cans coming back from the well, looking like queens in their colourful flowing robes, although they are as poor as beggars. The big eyes of the children with their lank hair and lice-infested clothes. The feeling of helplessness at the sight of the destinies of all this humanity. The disturbing mix of all the energy, the pulse, the confusion, the dirt and the sheer vastness of this city.

Although it is quiet now, there is no rest in me. Although I have escaped the mess of the city, my inner self is full of noise. Mumbai is in me.

TRAFFIC

Everyone who prays knows this, and it is a lesson that is never done. As soon as we try to be quiet, we realize how unquiet we are. All the busyness and cares of the day press in on us, all the impressions of the day linger on, suddenly it seems loud when the silence falls. During the day we're not even conscious of much of it. But how deeply pictures have become buried in us, how much an inner conflict smoulders, how driven and stressed you are; you can feel it all when you try to be quiet and to pray. The 'traffic' is in me. That is why there is no prayer life without the need to fight distraction. Maybe it's anticipated as comfort, or disillusionment. Distractions never disappear completely, even when you stay 'tuned in' for a long time. But there are important differences in how you handle it.

The first and most significant realization is simply this: we are distracted. It is shameful and revealing to recognize how much the things of the outside world persist in our inner self. When you begin to pray, cast a look around inside your own head. All that has been thrown in there in the last few days is there. First, there are the normal things of daily life. That I still need to change the tyres and have to call Aunt Anna – this just occurs to me when I try to pray. I may not have called Aunt Anna for years, but

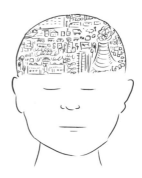

suddenly it seems to be of the highest urgency. A relationship conflict is still working in my heart and murmuring on. The day ahead comes to me worryingly with all its problems. As well as the matters of everyday life, however, we also seek out distractions and fill our brains with them: the news with all the global crises of humanity, the information on social media and music that sounds from all corners, practically all day and night, the advertising, pictures in films and magazines and video games.

The flood of impressions is not bad, *per se*, not forbidden. But it has an influence on our hearts. Once Jesus compared the human heart to arable soil, in which the good things of God can grow. Unfortunately, there are also thorns that grow tall there, and these can suffocate the good seed.

WEEDS GROW ALONE
YOU DON'T NEED TO WATER THORNS

What might these thorns be, that prevent the growth of God's word in the human heart? Perhaps you can think of the big and bad ones first. But instead, Jesus says:

'As for what was sown among thorns, this is the one who hears the word, but the cares of the world and the deceitfulness of riches choke the word, and it proves unfruitful.'

MATTHEW 13:22 ESV

What are the thorns? They are the worries of this world, and earning money. Now, money is not bad, it is more about what you do with it. Worries are in themselves also a natural part of life, but we should not let them go wild. For a few years my family and I have had a small garden at the front of our house, and I have learned something: you should not water weeds. Thorns grow by themselves and when there is nothing to hold them back, weeds take over the whole garden. This picture can be applied to our 'inner garden'. By themselves, cares and concerns about material things (money) and distractions will keep coming. Thorns grow by themselves, you do not have to water them. But, if you want God's word to grow in your heart, you have to take decisive steps. And sometimes a strimmer helps too.

Traffic in your head is normal, but it prevents the encounter. One day, Jesus and his disciples were the guests of Mary and Martha, who he had developed a close friendship with. Mary sat at the feet of Jesus and listened to him. But Martha was completely stressed and busy entertaining the guests. She was so busy that she didn't have time for Jesus himself. His word to her is amazingly clear:

IF YOU WANT GOD'S WORD TO GROW IN YOUR HEART, YOU HAVE TO TAKE DECISIVE STEPS. AND SOMETIMES A STRIMMER HELPS TOO.

'Martha, Martha, you are anxious and troubled about many things, but one thing is necessary. Mary has chosen the good portion, which will not be taken away from her.'

LUKE 10:41–42 ESV

Jesus did not mean it was wrong for Martha to want to care for their needs. Rather, in every relationship we need to take time to just simply give our full attention to one another. Just as in a marriage where, without time spent just being together it will not thrive, so a relationship with Jesus will not grow without time 'at his feet'. There will never come a day where there are no distractions. There are reasons enough to lose ourselves in activity. But then we also lose the depth and beauty of life. The true source is always the presence of Jesus.

But how, in practical terms, can we deal with distraction? What can you do when your thoughts constantly wander? One possibility would be to actively shut them off. If a thought comes, you send it away. The problem with this method is that you have to constantly deal with distractions yourself. A pretty tedious business. This prayer time is like the computer game, Space Invaders; the one who prays is always on the lookout for distractions flying past to shoot them with his mental shotgun.

This technique is not very helpful because the thoughts keep coming back, and the more attention you give to fighting them, the more attention and time they receive. There is a simpler, more elegant solution that points in another direction. Imagine you are sitting on a river bank. On the river, large and small ships pass by. Each one of them bears the name of a distraction. On the horizon, for example, 'shopping list for tomorrow' emerges, or 'roof insulation' or any other subject. The natural tendency is to jump aboard this ship and actively think about this subject. So, go through the shopping list and think about what you have forgotten. Or ponder how to solve the problem of the roof. Once you jump on the ship, it takes a little time and effort to get off the boat again. Before you realize it, you have lost ten minutes in pondering the various considerations in front of you, but the encounter with Jesus has eluded you.

Now, there is another way to deal with the passing ships. Very important: you do not have to fight them. You can't, anyway. They may come and go, but they should just sail by. You must not jump on board. Sit relaxed on the shore, Jesus next to you. After the prayer time there will be opportunity enough to think through these things. But for now 'only one thing is needed'. Sometimes it can help to write down the distraction on a piece of paper and 'lay it down' there. So our subconscious mind knows that the question is not forgotten, even if that ship has passed by.

PRACTICE
EXERCISE 1

I'm afraid it takes a little time to become quiet in your inner self. That is why today's first exercise is a little more challenging. It all hangs on the fact that the prayer time is longer. It should be sixty minutes today. The previous exercises have shown a number of possibilities as to how to fill this hour. Entering into the 'here and now'. Becoming fully aware of yourself and your surroundings. Praying the stations with the inner picture of the temple, or with the individual requests of the Lord's prayer. The goal is simple – to spend an entire hour in prayer. The challenge of distractions will really be felt now. But with the help of the image of the passing ships, it is worth a try.

Basically, there is no prescribed length of time for how long we should pray. But as human beings we usually need a certain amount of time to really immerse ourselves in something. No one runs a warm bath full of bubbles only to stay in it for thirty seconds. Or prepares a romantic candlelit dinner and only allows seven minutes to enjoy it. The question is not how long we *should* pray for, but how long we need to enter in to the here and now, and to leave behind distractions. Today's exercise encourages you, this time, to try an hour.

EXERCISE 2

The degree of distraction that one encounters in prayer depends on how much distraction you are exposed to in general. A few further exercises might be worth trying:

- A day with no media. No TV, no music, no newspaper and no social networks. Just try it.
- Holidays without internet. For the younger generation this may be hard to imagine, but it is extremely rewarding. A weekend, or two weeks, without mobile phones, computers and internet. I tried it myself and it was great!
- Try driving without the radio on, and in this way giving your head a little time without any input.
- Limit your time on the internet and consciously make the last hour before bedtime free of media. Allow your mind to rest, and do not fill your sleep with an inordinate number of superfluous pictures.
- Fast for a day. The absence of food focusses the heart and increases the hunger for God. And do not worry, omitting one, two or three meals is by no means harmful to health.[3]

---

3 Further suggestions for fasting can be found in: Johannes Hartl, *Heart Fire*, (Muddy Pearl, 2018).

CHAPTER 10

SCRIPT

It has all been for nothing. Only now, here on the landing, does the exhaustion of the last few weeks hit him. It's just never good enough, in spite of all the effort. Frank throws his coat in the corner, the door clicks shut. It had been far too long a day. It hadn't started all that badly. He'd even managed a short prayer time with coffee this morning, and a Bible passage. He'd had a good feeling in the car and a sense of expectancy about the meeting. How many times had he gone through the presentation in his head? Prepared for every possible critical question in advance? But then, in the lift – to meet Baxter, of all people, with his constant cheerful smile. It just seemed that everything always went his way. 'Sales team,' thought Frank. 'What do they even need to know?' Unlike him, in the development team …

And then, the opening statement from the boss. Did he even notice him? The first presentation of the day, ironically, was Baxter's. My goodness, it all seems to come so easily to him. He just stood there and did it. In a conversational tone, his report on the state of the dealer contacts, the plans for optimizing customer service. It all sounded so reasonable, so confident. And of course everyone warmed to him. How they looked at him! He's only been in the company a few months! And then came Frank's presentation. Many weeks' worth of work, painstakingly compiling results. Proposals for a new product. A slightly changed physical material composition for the surface of the brake, to be exact. Somehow, Frank survived the agonizing ten minutes. Immediately after that: critical queries about the production, objections from the boss himself. Complaints from the chief executive. That was all too clear. There was one point he had not thought of; although the objections from the boss were rather unsupported, he was painfully aware of the difficulty in implementation that was mentioned.

In short, the presentation was a failure; his project had died. His work was in vain. Typical! No idea if his position in the company was still even secure. The others are just better. He just does not 'have it'. 'Murphy's law', a fellow student in college had always called it – everything that can go wrong, will go wrong. That is exactly how Frank feels when he throws his coat in the corner and wonders why he is even making any effort to do anything when the game is just unfair and in the end only young minions like Baxter earn their laurels.

'Yes, my day was fine, sweetheart,' he forces a weary smile. 'And yours?' His wife Daniela and their two daughters take their places at the kitchen table – a short prayer and then chilli con carne. At least the food is good. Then everything happens rather quickly. It gushes out of his daughter, Clarissa, like a shaken bottle of champagne. His eldest looks like Daniela, only taller and with more freckles.

'Mum, Dad, I have to tell you something,' she begins with sparkling eyes. 'I told you about Millie, who I met at summer camp?' she continues, still holding her fork and spoon. 'Yesterday we chatted and I asked her what she is doing after graduation. And you know what? She is going to Africa! There is a discipleship school in Rwanda, and they have really good missions in the bush and they are going into the villages and …' Clarissa puts her cutlery down, the food seems completely forgotten in her enthusiasm.

Frank and Daniela throw one another brief unsettled glances.

'And now you want to go to Africa, right?' Frank picks up, 'Training is not that important, is it?'

'Well yes, I think it's a great opportunity! For years I've done nothing but this stupid schoolwork, and now I really want to do something for God!'

'I understand that,' Daniela intervenes. 'But does it really have to be Africa?'

'You know, Clarissa, not everything in life is so easy. Nowadays working life is no picnic. Nothing is given to you on a plate!' Frank adds. Suddenly, his own day at the office returns to mind.

'But Dad, don't you always say that it's important to trust God?' Clarissa replied, now more certain of her side.

'Help yourself, then God will help you, I tell you, my dear girl. There are too many princesses out there who have never learned the true value of hard work.'

'But I want to find my vocation. Maybe I could stay in Africa and be a missionary?' Clarissa says, somewhere between defiance and supplication.

'And live on love and fresh air, is that it?' Frank asks, horrified.

'Or God's provision … ' Clarissa says, but Frank interrupts her: 'Real life looks very different. It is "Eat or be eaten". The job that you don't get will go to another. You can listen to pious stories as much as you like, but a sense of reality, just occasionally, would be helpful.' In his mind's eye it is now abundantly clear. All that struggle, all the grind and graft of the last few weeks. Bitter resentment sticks in his throat, while deep furrows dig into his brow.

'But what if it's my dream?' Clarissa hurls back, full of outrage.

'Your dream? Grow up, will you! That is nothing but pure fantasy.' Frank throws his napkin on the table, and with an outstretched finger pointing at Clarissa, he adds, 'Remember one thing. There is nothing in life that you can rely on. Except that everything that can go wrong, actually will go wrong.'

Pause. Silence. Disconcerted and horrified, Clarissa stares at her father. 'Do you even know what you just said?' Shaking her head as if she simply can't believe it, she asks, 'What has happened to you?' and jumps up, rushing from the room.

SCRIPT

Script. The name of a prescribed procedure. There might be, for example, a script for a lecture or a script for the stage. But there are also internal scripts. At least, this is what some psychologists call certain deep-seated processes in the mind: thought structures. You don't usually meet them head on, only in certain situations. Only when his daughter informed him about her plans to go abroad, did it become apparent what thoughts would automatically appear in Frank's head. These are thoughts and beliefs which we usually acquire early on, passed on by our parents. The problem is, that by no means do these beliefs necessarily correspond to the truth. Even people who, like Frank, are actually Christians, are confronted with mental scripts, even sometimes convincing ones, which are contrary to biblical truth about the nature of God.

What does this have to do with prayer? Everything. Because it is exactly here that we immerse ourselves into these thought patterns. Only when all outer noise dies down, do you realize all that is going on in your head. Our inner script may be founded on a previous situation, for example. 'It was clear, yet again, no one was interested in me.' The thought echoes inside, even though the embarrassing encounter with the relatives is long over. This is the starting point for what Paul describes as an essential element of a healthy inner life:

> Do not conform to the pattern of this world, but be
> transformed by the renewing of your mind. Then you will
> be able to test and approve what God's will is – his good,
> pleasing and perfect will.

ROMANS 12:2

This point deserves careful consideration. First of all, something has to happen so that we can test and discern what the will of God is. It is not always what we think. Not everything that we assume about God and his plans is in accordance with the truth. To be able to judge correctly, an inner transformation is needed. But this happens through the renewing of your mind.

Frank believes in God, but his inner script is full of statements. For instance, the performance-oriented, 'It's never good enough'; or the despondent, 'It achieves nothing'; or the envious, 'It's easy for everyone else'; or the profoundly unbelieving, 'God helps those who help themselves', which actually implies that nobody helps you, you have to do it all yourself. In fact, in our thought lives we are deciding constantly between whether to follow a script of belief or unbelief, thanks or envy, praise or problems, trust or self-sufficiency. So now let's turn to that.

NOT EVERYTHING THAT WE ASSUME ABOUT GOD AND HIS PLANS IS IN ACCORDANCE WITH THE TRUTH. TO BE ABLE TO JUDGE CORRECTLY, AN INNER TRANSFORMATION IS NEEDED.

FAITH OR UNBELIEF

Any life situation can be seen through the lens of trust in God, or that of refusal to trust. In every situation either faith or unbelief can gain the upper hand. All too easily, what we believe about God and his plans can be pushed out of kilter with truth. To judge rightly, an inner transformation is required. All too easily, we put the responsibility on the circumstances: in such difficult situations, or surrounded by such unpleasant people, we can't help but despair. That, however, is a lie. Although we can't always change our circumstances, how we react to them is always our responsibility.

What pronouncements reign in my mind about my workplace, my wife, my children, life in general? 'My boss is unfair,' 'She will never change,' 'This kid is just lazy and will amount to nothing,' 'It's all going to pot,' are statements that express an unbelief in God's ability to change a situation. God is faithful, he has good intentions, and he is omnipotent! To what extent does truth characterize your thinking in these practical areas?

THANKFULNESS VERSUS ENVY

There are always good reasons to be envious. It will not be long before you discover there are things you do not have; or before you meet people who are more popular, more successful, prettier and richer than you are yourself. Envy is a fundamental attitude of the heart which poisons everything – and by the way it is very common in our society. The Bible reports that the first murder of human history was due to envy (Genesis 4:1–16). The problem is that the causes of envy never disappear from the world. There will always be someone who can do something better than you, or who has more than you. Envy does not just eat the goodwill between people, it also destroys the joy in what you see, have and know.

If envy dominates the heart, then it is also reflected in the 'inner script'. Unfortunately, one does not achieve right-mindedness without going deeper; it requires a real turnaround and decision against it. The next step is to put a new, healthy script in place of the old one. The antidote to envy is gratitude. Anyone who is thankful for what he has, does not take it for granted. He turns his attention away from what he does not have, to what he can enjoy. He turns his attention to the goodness and generosity of God and away from want. So, build thankfulness into your thought life (thanking and thinking belong together). This helps to rid the heart of envy.

Which people do you look at with envy? What good things do you notice only rarely? Which persons or aspects of your life could you give more appreciative attention or grateful thanksgiving to?

PRAISE VERSUS PROBLEM ORIENTATION

There are some situations in life where a problem becomes so over-whelming that one can't think about anything else. But when there is no significant problem, our thoughts often revolve around the negative for much of the time. Our inner eye is captivated by the size and significance of a conflict, a worry, a difficulty. Everything centres on this. But prayer in general is the ceasing of the human heart from circling around itself, and instead fixating towards God (see also chapter 8). Praise means saying how God is. Making him the centre of your atten-tion. 'God is omnipotent' means exactly that: no problem is greater than he. 'God is good' means:

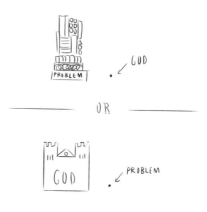

no circumstance can change the fact that there is a good plan for my life here.

What are you more impressed by: God himself, or your problem? Matthew's Gospel tells a moving story about just this. Jesus' disciples are in the boat when a violent storm hits. Suddenly they see Jesus walking across the lake. Visibly impressed, Peter asks if, on the word of Jesus, he too might walk across the water to Jesus. And it works, for a few steps. 'But when he saw the wind, he was afraid and, beginning to sink, cried out, "Lord, save me!"' (Matthew 14:30). This is important! Of course, Peter had already noticed how fierce the wind and waves were before this. But as long as, in the middle it all, his eyes were on Jesus, he could walk on the water. This shows that faith is instrumental in our focus. What am I looking at? If my attention is completely taken up with problems, I will sink into them. However, if my inner eye stays on Jesus, despite the storm, a completely new path will suddenly emerge.

Are there statements of praise inside you or are there only statements about the size of the almighty problem?

TRUST VERSUS SELF-SUFFICIENCY

The Bible describes this as the first and fundamental problem of man. Trusting in the fact that God intends good for us first surfaces as a problem in the Garden of Eden. It seemed much better to take the extended hand of the tree of knowledge rather than risk being taken in. Beliefs such as 'God is my Father' or 'The Lord is my Shepherd' often stand oddly in conflict with what we actually really think. 'It's all down to me,' 'Nothing in life is ever free,' 'He who relies on others will be let down' – this stubborn clinging to wanting to be self-sufficient reveals a deep-seated refusal to really trust.

The thought of being able to control our lives is quite obviously a delusion. The most existential things of life remain unplannable. Jesus asks:

'Who of you by worrying can add a single hour to your life? Since you cannot do this very little thing, why do you worry about the rest?'

LUKE 12:25–26

And yet, worrying and self-reliance run deep. Repentance, the turning back towards trust, must be redone daily and hourly. The inner script in our minds is the place of decision.

How well do you manage to let go? In which situations in your life do you find it hard to give God authority?

RENEWAL OF THE MIND

The transformation of our thinking is a tedious but necessary process. A part of it can't be done alone. We need good theology and doctrine, correction by others and fellowship with other mature Christians. Sometimes we need therapy. Often, only through contact with other people, in work situations or relationships, is it clear how untransformed our thinking really is. This realization may be hard, but after all it is much worse not to realize how much of our way is still ahead.

Prayer is not primarily about our thinking. To have a healthy prayer life one also has to handle the word of God. And that has the capacity to change our thinking, in fact, even to put it to the test:

For the word of God is alive and active. Sharper than any double-edged sword, it penetrates even to dividing soul and spirit, joints and marrow; it judges the thoughts and attitudes of the heart.

HEBREWS 4:12

The very important statement in this biblical passage is not that the mind judges the word of God ('I can't imagine that, that's why it can't be true'), but that the word of God judges the mind! At the same time, it is powerful: it does not just speak in abstract terms, but it does what it says (see also Isaiah 55:10–11). And it becomes tangible.

THE WORD OF GOD HAS THE CAPACITY TO CHANGE OUR THINKING, IN FACT, EVEN TO PUT IT TO THE TEST.

PRACTICE

EXERCISE 1

I encourage you to read a passage in the Bible and apply it to your thinking. This means not just to stop at reading ('That's very interesting, what it says there'), but to apply your thinking to a decision, and to seal this in prayer. And it's best to put it in writing.

In practice, the way to do this is to pick up a Bible and a notebook and begin with a passage from the New Testament or the Psalms. Read until you find a sentence that makes something resonate inside you or fits with the current situation. Write this sentence in the notebook. Now pray with this phrase by phrase:

- Thank God it is true.
- Ask God to tell you more about this truth.
- Decide to believe this statement as true.
- If possible, decide on some concrete steps, to live out this truth accordingly.

For example, in a situation where you feel lonely, you might come across Psalm 145:18 which says, 'The Lord is near to all who call on him, to all who call on him in truth.'

The exercise described above could look like this in your notebook:

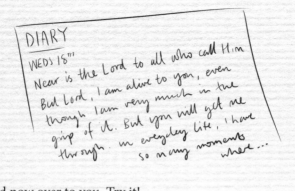

And now over to you. Try it!

EXERCISE 2

Everyone encounters lies in their thought life. Below is a list of especially popular false statements that shape many of our inner scripts. Maybe not at first glance, but if you look deeper into yourself, they may sound familiar. By contrast, I set the appropriate biblical truth. In the course of one or more of your prayer times, you can go through this list and see which lies you encounter in your thinking. You can apply the truth that lies next to it, as I have described in Exercise 1. Of course, there are many other suitable Bible verses. You can research for yourself which verse you want to use to oppose your inner lies.

LIE:
'Nobody cares about me.'

TRUTH:
But the eyes of the LORD are on those
who fear him,
on those whose hope is in his
unfailing love,
to deliver them from death
and keep them alive in famine.
PSALM 33:18–19

LIE:
'I have to be perfect.'

TRUTH:
... the LORD is compassionate and
gracious, slow to anger, abounding in love.
PSALM 103:8

LIE:

'I'm powerless.'

TRUTH:

The Spirit you received does not make you slaves, so that you live in fear again; rather, the Spirit you received brought about your adoption to sonship. And by him we cry, 'Abba, Father.'
ROMANS 8:15

LIE:

'It's always the same old story, everything goes wrong.'

TRUTH:

And we know that in all things God works for the good of those who love him, who have been called according to his purpose.
ROMANS 8:28

LIE:

'It's easier to avoid problems than to face them.'

TRUTH:

I can do all this through him who gives me strength.
PHILIPPIANS 4:13

LIE:

'If God does not live up to my expectations, he probably does not love me.'

TRUTH:

For our light and momentary troubles are achieving for us an eternal glory that far outweighs them all. So we fix our eyes not on what is seen, but on what is unseen, since what is seen is temporary, but what is unseen is eternal.
2 CORINTHIANS 4:17–18

LIE:

'Somebody else is to blame.'

TRUTH:

If we claim to be without sin we deceive ourselves and the truth is not in us. If we confess our sins, he is faithful and just and will forgive us our sins and purify us from all righteousness.
1 JOHN 1:8–9

LIE:

'I can't be happy if everything does not go the way I want it to be.'

TRUTH:

Though an army besiege me,
my heart will not fear;
though war break out against me,
even then I will be confident.
PSALM 27:3

LIE:

'You have to earn God's love.'

TRUTH:

For it is by grace you have been saved, through faith – and this is not from yourselves, it is the gift of God – not by works, so that no one can boast.
EPHESIANS 2:8–9

LIE:

'God hates sin and the sinner.'

TRUTH:

But God demonstrates his own love for us in this: while we were still sinners, Christ died for us.
ROMANS 5:8

LIE:

'It is my duty to fulfil everyone's expectations.'

TRUTH:

Am I now trying to win the approval of human beings, or of God? Or am I trying to please people? If I were still trying to please people, I would not be a servant of Christ.
GALATIANS 1:10

LIE:

'It will never get better for me. I just do not expect to change.'

TRUTH:

... being confident of this, that he who began a good work in you will carry it on to completion until the day of Christ Jesus.
PHILIPPIANS 1:6

LIE:

'God will save me from all evil.'

TRUTH:

Who shall separate us from the love of Christ? Shall trouble or hardship or persecution or famine or nakedness or danger or sword? As it is written:
'For your sake we face death all day long;
we are considered as sheep to be slaughtered.'
No, in all these things we are more than conquerors through him who loved us.
ROMANS 8:35–37

LIE:

'A good Christian is never angry, depressed, worried.'

TRUTH:

Come to me, all you who are weary and burdened, and I will give you rest.
MATTHEW 11:28

CHAPTER 11

VOICE

The May sunshine on my back. Thousands of insects buzz around me as I climb up through the long grass of the fragrant meadow. In the forest it's cooler and the ground is damp. Over roots and stony steps, the path leads me to the almshouse, close to the summit. Many hours have gone by since I arrived in the valley below. Since the car brought me here to Allgäu from the loud world of the city. Into the nothingness. Into the cowbell and lily-of-the-valley-nothingness. Into the great silence, which since then has woven around me like bales of thick fabric. A leisurely pace, ever higher. Walking slowly, like someone who doesn't have to be anywhere.

It took me more than a day just to get here. At first, my thoughts were ROARING. The needs, the expectations, the opinions. All those voices. Involved in a public debate in the last few days, and the voices of the critics, those who say I'm wrong, still echo afterwards. Just like the voices of praise; something like this needed to be said urgently. It had all started with a Facebook post. Suddenly it was in a newspaper and then emerged on several online platforms. I gave interviews about it. Not comparable to what politicians experience daily, but for me, quite exciting. In the middle of the voice-storms, I made my departure into the nothingness that I described in chapter 1. Offline. The uncertainty of how the debate would progress in the meantime. Of who else might speak or add their voice.

Yet a few days later, it has all blown over. Far below me, the hazy valley, and ahead the majestic mountain ranges in the bright azure of noon. Step by step, and up and up, the path leads me onward. And inside, in the great calm of the forest, suddenly the voice. In the silence of my evenly beating, wandering heart, the word within. Words that were not there in me before are brought to me like food. Words that do not come from outside, like a snatched phrase. Words that fall inside me like a heavy stone into deep water. Not by my own conviction and decision, but by their own weight, they sink to the bottom. And they stay there. It is the voice. I know you. It is as familiar to me as the voice of a friend, but so different, so foreign, so unattainable. I follow this voice. It draws me. I've missed it a hundredfold; I had forgotten. For months it has been supplanted by my own monologue. But today, it meets me again, up here in the high air. Up here in the shady forest where the birds are singing. It's just a few words. Words of reminder. Words of direction. Course correction. New priorities. But it changes everything, this voice. As I descend, I take a different way. It takes me home quickly and safely. In my heart, the voice sounds. The voice that is different from all others.

VOICE

God speaks. Not only is the Bible full of stories of the men and women that God spoke to, but beyond that, Jesus seems completely without doubt in assuming that his disciples can hear his voice.

> *My sheep listen to my voice; I know them, and they follow me.*

JOHN 10:27

There is clearly no question as to whether God wants to talk with us and that he is able to. What is unclear is only whether we rely on talking with God, whether we give his voice room and learn to differentiate it from all others.

All human history stands and falls on the question of whose voice you listen to. In the story of the Fall in the Old Testament, the tempter approaches Eve by speaking to her. It was by no means a given that she would listen; many other methods of seduction would have been possible. But in the Eden narrative the serpent speaks. The problem is, Eve hears him. And all evil springs from there. God has said to man that he may eat from any of the trees in the garden, with the exception of one: the tree of knowledge of good and evil. Man can't arbitrarily determine what is good and what is evil. If he attempts to moderate this himself, things always go completely wrong. The horrible ideologies of the twentieth century are a powerful demonstration of what happens if a leader or revolutionary faction tries to define good and evil for all, even ultimately whose life is worth living and whose death is acceptable.

Humankind receives from God a garden full of delicious fruit trees, at their disposal. Adam and Eve lack nothing, they have everything they need. But the voice of the tempter awakens her imagination. How good would it be to taste the fruit of the forbidden tree?! How about trying it just once? And when Eve listens to the snake, that central, blunt lie finally grabs her:

'You will not certainly die,'
the snake said to the woman.
'For God knows that when
you eat from it your eyes will
be opened, and you will be
like God, knowing good and
evil.'

THERE
SHE
SAW

GENESIS 3:4-5

In other words, God is a liar! He begrudges you all happiness. He is not for you!

What is amazing, is what the Scripture goes on to say in the next verse:

> When the woman saw that the fruit of the tree was good for food and pleasing to the eye, and also desirable for gaining wisdom ...
>
> GENESIS 3:6a

Eve sees only this one tree. Her eyes are captivated. Suddenly all the delicious fruits on all the other trees are forgotten. But apparently this happens only now, after she has listened to the voice of the devil.

Which voices we choose to heed is crucial. Because that will decide what we see and what we desire. Just as we have physical eyes, there are also spiritual eyes, that is, the eyes of faith. But faith, as we read in Paul, comes from hearing (Romans 10:17). Because the voice that the ear inclines to, determines the perception. And that became Eve's undoing. Only when she listened to the wrong voice did she begin to see the forbidden tree as desirable.

'I only believe what I see,' is how the contemporary materialistic worldview puts it. But that is not true. Because often you do not see what you do not want to see. So probably the statement should be, more accurately, 'I only see what I believe.' And what one believes is inseparably entwined with whose voice one listens to.

God speaks to us in many ways. The beauty of nature and the fact that 'there is something and not nothing,'[4] in itself speaks of a Creator. And ultimately, God speaks in one binding and unsurpassable way, and that is

WHICH VOICES WE CHOOSE TO HEED IS CRUCIAL. BECAUSE THAT WILL DECIDE WHAT WE SEE AND WHAT WE DESIRE.

4 Author's paraphrase of Gottfried Wilhelm Leibniz in *Principle of Sufficient Reason.*

through his Son, Jesus Christ. Jesus was not just a prophet, he himself is the Word of God (John 1:1); he is not just a messenger, he himself is the message. This message of God about himself has found expression in the writings of the Bible – the same Bible that was written through the inspiration of the Holy Spirit. Jesus is the Word of God, the books of Scripture announce him infallibly. But this chapter is about a fact that many Christians are not very familiar with themselves. It is about God speaking in the heart of man.

Just as there are different 'inner looks' there are also inner voices. We can assign to them the same kinds of roles, just as we did for looks. The inner script, the different voices in our head and inner looks all present us with the same challenge in the end. To be led by God and not by the fantasies or the ideas of people. God speaks to us. But how does one distinguish his voice from others? And how can we learn to hear them better?

For hundreds of years, writers on the spiritual life have typical names for the voice of God. Personally, the following have been especially helpful to me. They are of value only if seen together in some combination. The voice of God …

1. A BREAKING-IN TO THE ROUTINE.

THOUGHTS – ROUTINE

An average train of thought might look something like this: I look out of the window and see the hedge, which still needs to be cut, but wonder if it might be about to rain. This makes me worried about the weather, because the barbeque is tomorrow. I think of Sandra and Alexander, who are also invited. I wonder for a bit, whether there is something between the two of them. It would be funny if the two of them got married. That's when I remember a wedding from last August when it was so hot. And right after that we went on holiday. And now I remember the hot Croatian coast and the island-rich sea. And the traffic jam on the motorway. Now suddenly the statement, 'I am with you, do not be afraid,' drops into my head. And he has my attention. Because the first characteristic of God's voice is that there is suddenly something new, strange and unexpected.

2. IT HAS A SPECIAL QUALITY.

Every voice has its own sound. Some voices resolve something in us, just from our hearing them. When someone speaks they are recognized not just by the words they say, but also by the sound. The voice of God has a special quality. God's voice has a special character that anyone who has heard it before will recognize. I call it the 'wow-feeling'. It is unlike anything else that happens in your mind. In his letter to the Galatians Paul describes the 'fruit of the spirit', that is the effect of the Holy Spirit on the heart – 'love, joy, peace, patience, kindness, goodness, faithfulness, gentleness, self-control.' (Galatians 5:22–23 ESV). The inner voice, then, that leaves a taste of freedom and joy tends to be from God. The voice of evil, on the other hand, always has the taste of fear, coercion, pressure and lack of freedom. The Holy Spirit always shows opportunities and options for action, never forcing just one, or narrowing the options.

3. REMAINS.

The normal train of thought continues to flow quickly. Thoughts come and go. Voices often die away very quickly. God is the faithful one, who always stays the same. An impression that is of God reverberates and usually becomes even stronger over time. When it is about a life

RED THREAD

choice or taking a big step, God usually talks about it over a long period of time. There will be several impressions. Often you can recognize the track of the voice of God as a red thread that moves through life for months and years. Whatever comes to mind when you are praying and in the presence of God, that should be taken seriously.

4. CONSISTENT.

The same God who speaks to us through Scripture, is the God we are able to communicate with today. But in God there is no contradiction. He says nothing today which contradicts his nature, or what he said yesterday. That's why a real word from God cannot disagree with the Bible. Even supernatural phenomena, or mystical experiences, are to be rejected if they

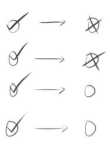

are not in accordance with the New Testament and the teaching of the church. Speaking unusually sharply, Paul says:

> *But even if we or an angel from heaven should preach a gospel other than the one we preached to you, let them be under God's curse!*

GALATIANS 1:8

God doesn't contradict himself. And in distinguishing the voices, the most important question is whether or not they agree with the word of God.

Very often, there will be correspondences with the earlier impressions of a spiritually mature Christian or a pastor.

5. BRINGS INNER PEACE.

Many thoughts sound good at first. Only through the consequences do we recognize the rotten root. The best example of this is, once more, Adam and Eve. After eating the fruit, they did not become like God but were driven out of the garden and became mortal. If we follow the voice of God, then we will have lasting peace. Even when it comes to giving up something that is dear to us, or something that is

challenging to do, there remains a peace in the heart, compensating for it all. Especially so when it concerns a calling in our lives. So, in choosing a job or a relationship or the whole direction of life, it is a question of utmost significance as to whether deep inner peace sets in. If this continues to be absent, we can assume that we have misheard, misunderstood, not yet sought or deliberately rejected God's voice.

If all five criteria are met, there is a high probability that we have heard the voice of God. In fact, it is only a high probability, never wholly certain. There is no one who always hears God's voice without doubt and can distinguish it without error (see 1 Corinthians 13:9). Sometimes you just have to dare to go and do something. Peter didn't know that the water would support him until he set foot out of the boat and walked towards Jesus. (Matthew 14:29). Precisely because we are fallible, we need the feedback of other people. And the willingness to turn around, if perhaps it turns out to be the wrong the way. But God rewards steps of obedience, and the ability to hear his voice increases each time when we give it room and obey.

PETER DIDN'T KNOW THAT THE WATER WOULD SUPPORT HIM UNTIL HE SET FOOT OUT OF THE BOAT AND WALKED TOWARDS JESUS.

The following factors help us to hear the voice of God:[5]

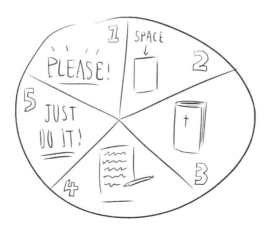

5 I talk about some of these in my book, *Heart Fire*.

1. PRAY SPECIFICALLY!

God loves it when we ask him specifically for something. We do not receive much, because we do not ask (James 4:2). How many meetings and arguments have I stumbled into, without asking God for his words? And how many times have I received a decisive idea in prayer, that was better than anything I could have thought of myself? You need wisdom in your job, in your family, in a difficult situation. Ask him to speak specifically.

2. MAKE ROOM!

But then take the time to hear if an answer is coming. It will not always come, and not always immediately. The exercises in this book contain many suggestions as to how to increase the silence in your life. The less your head is filled with other voices, the easier you will find it to hear his voice. Some silence and switching off makes it a lot easier to hear the gentle voice of God.

3. READ THE BIBLE!

Anyone who knows God's written word well can also recognize his spoken voice more easily. Very often God uses the individual sentences of the Bible to speak specifically to us.

4. WRITE IT DOWN!

At home I have a little book, in which, over twenty years ago, I began to write down prophetic impressions and words. They are a treasure which I like to fall back on, for God's handwriting is clearly visible. You remember things better when you write them down. And in retrospect, written notes are a wonderful aid to learning to distinguish God's word over a long period of time.

5. ACT OBEDIENT!

Do you feel a sudden impulse to invite a homeless person to dinner? Or to tell a work colleague about Jesus? Or to donate money to someone? Or to say something special to your children? And do these inclinations agree with the above criteria? Then do it! Yes, the danger is that you might be wrong, but you can learn from your mistakes. You will grow into hearing God's voice. And the success rate increases the more you do it. I myself have had some embarrassing experiences in this, but many more real miracles.[6]

6 I describe some of these experiences in my book *Heart Fire*.

PRACTICE

The five points just mentioned are suitable for a simple prayer time. Take a Bible and writing materials. Find a place where you will be undisturbed and make time and space for God to speak. Ask him specifically for his word on a specific topic, and listen. When a thought comes to you, write it down. If nothing comes, it doesn't matter. Just the attitude of listening itself, is an attitude of love which pleases God. Read a passage from the Bible and ask God to come and speak to you through his word. At the end, give him back this prayer time without trying to evaluate yourself whether it was good or not. Whether you have heard something or not, the more you ask and listen attentively, the more often you will hear his voice. And that changes everything.

CHAPTER 12

RHYTHM 168

The sun shines brightly over the fields. What a magnificent blue sky! The weather forecast was right, thinks Alfred the farmer, on taking an early morning look out of the window. Today is the day, at last. The perfect day. The grain is ripe and healthy, the ears abundant and lush, and the harvest promises great things. The work awaits, there can be no delay. So, get everything ready quickly, because it might rain tomorrow. First things first: wash and dress. A quick coffee on the run. Where are those wellington boots? Not in the wardrobe, nor next to the tiled stove. Oh there, behind the cupboard in the hallway. Alfred opens the door and is suddenly holding the latch loose in his hand. Such a hassle! Quickly down to the basement to fetch the tools. It will only take a moment.

Behind the kitchen, a dark corridor leads to the cellar door. Alfred is just about to swing it open when his foot gets stuck on something and he almost falls. Darn! That was the phone cord. The jack is now hanging down, the wires dangling from the wall. 'I will have to call the electrician!' he thinks, annoyed, and rummages in the deep pockets of his work trousers for his mobile phone. But wait, it's still too early for the electrician. And the battery is flat. So, get the power lead from the kitchen. It must be somewhere in this drawer ... between stamps, a pocket knife, foil and a piece of string – but instead, here is the bill from the dentist, which was due two weeks ago! This payment must be made, urgently. He picks up a pen from the kitchen table and ... but who is that under the corner bench? That lazy tomcat Mikey. He is actually not allowed in the house.

'Mikey, get out with you!' He shouts sternly, but the peacefully purring pile of fur doesn't move one bit. So he carries Mikey outside. The newspaper has just come and is right there on the doormat. Just a quick glance – the commercial pages are such rubbish. Who needs all this advertising? Alfred bends down and takes the paper to the green bin. Isn't it bin day today? Yes, so he has to push the bin out front into the street. What is this here? Rubbish just thrown carelessly into the hedge? The hedge, which actually needs cutting urgently. Alfred decides to go to the garage and get the hedge trimmer. And so it goes on and on and on. When, finally, it is night, the phone is still not fixed, the bill still not paid and the field still not mown.

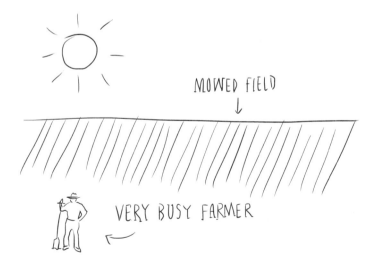

RHYTHM 168

Rhythm 168. Or the lack of it. We all laugh at the slightly chaotic farmer, Alfred. But doesn't he seem strangely familiar? The problem is always the same. There are always many things that cry out to be dealt with immediately. The day never comes when there will be nothing unforeseen, no spontaneous problems and no seemingly extremely urgent reasons not to do what one actually should be doing right now. If you don't want to end up like farmer Alfred, it is vital to learn the distinction between 'urgent' and 'important'.

There are tasks that are urgent, which means they need to be done immediately. However, not all of these tasks are also important. 'Important' means they have a long term decisive impact on your whole life.

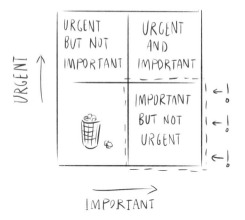

A text message lights up your mobile phone. The content is really not significant, but the effect is usually to prompt us to write back immediately. The mozzarella in the fridge will go off today and must be cooked urgently. The happiness of the whole world doesn't depend on this, but it is something that needs to be thought of today. Unfortunately, you will never be free of the unimportant, urgent things, but the time you give to them must be restricted. Otherwise there won't be enough time for the things which are important but not urgent. Regular cancer screening can be the difference between life and death. Yet, the sessions are not urgent. To give time to your spouse and children, to actively listen to them, is of the utmost importance for a healthy family. But this will usually only become urgent when there is a real crisis. And then, of course, there are things that are neither important nor urgent. These are pure distraction.

What is important and urgent must have priority. In second place come the activities that are important, but not urgent. The problem is that they will not put themselves forward on their own. They must be actively scheduled in, otherwise they will be missed. But a life under the dictatorship of the urgent will be fruitless and rushed.

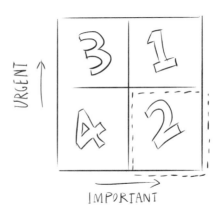

In the sketch, the spiritual life belongs in square '2' – important not urgent matters. Of course, not only that, but also:

- time for family
- health
- involvement in church and community
- education
- friendships.

As a little exercise to think through, in your head quickly assign your activities of the last four weeks to one of the four quadrants.

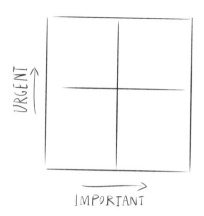

Prayer is not everything. But without prayer, everything is nothing. A daily routine where prayer is missing will be flat and dull. That's why this book is concerned with learning to pray and having a rhythm of prayer incorporated into daily life. It will influence everything else. It's about the realization that prayer, like every other important, non-urgent activity, has to be planned.

Anyone who wants to improve their physical fitness needs a definite plan. Something like, 'Tuesday, go to the gym; Friday, volleyball at 6pm'. The same applies to learning an instrument or a foreign language. You don't learn Italian by eating in a pizzeria. Nor by just spending time with people who speak Italian. No one would contemplate such an idea. But when it comes to our prayer lives, more than

A DAILY ROUTINE WHERE PRAYER IS MISSING WILL BE FLAT AND DULL.

a few people seem inclined to adopt this astonishing attitude. A spiritual experience alone ('I walked the way of St James and felt so close to heaven there'), or the regular attendance of worship services is no guarantee that you will grow in your spiritual life.

A look at your diary will allow you to recognize something that you may not have noticed. Everyone has about the same amount of time. And we take time for what is really important to us. No

YOU HAVE TIME FOR
WHAT IS IMPORTANT
TO YOU

one has ever yet starved because he or she lacked the time to eat. Anyone who is in love spends time with their beloved. When Jutta and I were a very young couple and living a long way apart, telephone calls were extremely expensive. But at night, between 2am and 5am, there was the so-called 'moonlight tariff' (who still remembers this term?). What did we do? Of course we set the alarm clock for 4am, to be able to talk on the phone for an hour! Love finds a way, and we usually find time for what is important to us. If something is supposedly important to us, but doesn't turn up regularly in the diary, this indicates that while that thing may be an intention, it is not yet a reality. If it is just a plan to be sportier, the dream of a six-pack will soon give way to a beer belly. And exactly the same thing applies to our prayer life.

168

Not everyone has an automatic association with this number. For us in the House of Prayer, it is the most essential number, because this is how many hours in a week people pray and sing in our prayer room. A week has 168 hours. Every single one. You might also say that everyone has exactly the same number of hours in a week, but everyone uses them differently. Of course, not all these hours are freely available. Few people have a choice as to whether they want to work or not. And absolutely no human being can rationalize away the need for sleep.

However, we tend to underestimate the potential amount of spare time that we actually have. A quick calculation: the average person works forty hours a week. Our average sleep requirement is a little under eight hours a day. If one adds the two together it gives a total of ninety-six hours. Two hours a day for meals and an hour for personal care, is also about average. With an hour for travel per day, for five working days, as well as two hours with family and two hours twice a week each for sports or friends. What do we have?

We have twenty-eight hours. Not a small number. That is four hours a day! There is a slight trick in this calculation, in that it treats weekdays and weekends alike. But of course our free time is not usually distributed evenly throughout the week. Nevertheless, what this is all about is the realization that we have more time than we think. It is simply not true that our time is fixed and we can't do anything about it. We always take time for what is most important to us.

Your personal spiritual life should be of the highest priority to you. This is clear from a little story about a farmer who owned a goose with highly unusual properties. Every day it laid an egg of pure gold. Only one each day, but one for sure. The farmer could rely on it: every morning he found a little shining treasure in the goose's nest. All he had to do was feed the goose daily, to give her water and some exercise.

WE ALWAYS TAKE TIME FOR WHAT IS MOST IMPORTANT

So in this way, by and by, the farmer came into a considerable fortune. One day when he was on his way back to the barn, a thought occurred to him. Was it not tiresome to have to wait twenty-four hours for the next egg? How about having a lot more eggs at once and in one fell swoop? And he'd be much richer? There she sat in front of him, the happy chattering goose. The goose from which all the golden eggs came. All the eggs, it dawned on the farmer at once, are now inside the goose. How else did they get here? How about if one could just simply get them out? For that, of course he would have to open the goose. He felt a little sorry for the goose, but very quickly the thought of the profit tempted him more. With a quick stab of the knife, the white goose was killed. Then he quickly cut open the stomach!

The cruel scene won't be described here. Thankfully it's a fable anyway. But one thing is certain: the farmer had roast goose to eat for a few days, but otherwise he found nothing significant in the belly of the goose. At any rate, it was the end of the golden eggs.

You too have a goose that lays golden eggs. In this book it has been given different names: the here and now, where God lives; the inner garden; the temple; life under God's eye; your daily prayer time. If you cultivate these steadily, they will make your everyday life rich. Just like the goose that only needs to be fed, to lay a golden egg every day.

There are dull days in which, despite all the hustle and bustle and all the effort, nothing seems to run smoothly. These are usually the days when we start to neglect our communion with God and try and do it alone. But to renounce prayer time in favour of something else you feel you urgently need to do, is to slaughter the goose in the hope of getting the gold more quickly. Care for your spiritual life. Cultivate the inner garden. Feed the goose. Your prayer life will become deeper every day and your whole life will be richer.

PRACTICE

This book is coming to an end. Time to take some practical steps. Hopefully you have acquired a taste for what a well-structured prayer life can look like. From all the different methods you can now develop your own, or choose something different every day. But everything depends on you choosing a fixed time and place for daily prayer. You need something like this:

TIMETABLE

	SUN	MON	TUES	WEDS	THURS	FRI	SAT
7 00		PRAYER	PRAYER			PRAYER	
8 00							
9 00							PRAYER
10 00							
11 00		W	W		W	W	HOUSE
12 00	CHURCH	O	O	WORK	O	O	WORK
13 00		R	R	PRAYER			FAMILY
14 00					R	R	
15 00		K	K	WORK			TIME
16 00					K	K	
17 00							
18 00			CHILD			CHILD	
19 00		GYM	CARE	HOME	GYM	CARE	
20 00				GROUP	PRAYER		
21 00	PRAYER	READING					
22 00							

So, a plan of what your week looks like. Anything that you attempt to undertake will only become reality if you place it on a regular schedule. What does a normal week look like for you? When do you want to free up time for your spiritual life? I encourage you to be bold. Because I believe that, for the vast majority of people, it wouldn't be a problem to set aside an hour for God every day. If that seems too much to you, think about it; maybe there are one or more days in your week where a full hour would be possible. Other days the time might be shorter. Relax. Because pressure, rules and striving generally have little to do with the spiritual life. It is more a question of how you want to live. If you want a daily life that is filled with the presence of God, then a daily prayer time will be a decisive factor in this.

Once you have decided on the time and place, only one piece of advice remains: see the time through! There are phases in the spiritual life where your prayer time will be dry and God will seem far away. That is normal. God allows this so that we learn to pray, not only for the satisfaction of our feelings, but for his own sake. I don't promise that your daily prayer life will always be wonderful, or that your whole life will immediately change. But I guarantee that the long-term fruit of a steady and faithful prayer life is huge.

Start with your plan straight away. Don't forget: we take our time for that which is most important to us. And if you're not sure how you will manage everything else you have to do in the time you have left, then you can be quite confident in claiming the word of Jesus for you: 'But seek first his kingdom and his righteousness, and all these things will be given to you as well.' (Matthew 6:33).

EPILOGUE

The heavy, humid heat of the valley, under the scorching sun. The bare mountains tower all around, those heights with which ancient, sacred and disturbing legends are entwined. The silence of noon. Her sandals leave small clouds of dust on the sandy road. Otherwise she would go unnoticed. It is not a long way from the city to the well. Now, on the way out, the clay pot on her shoulder is still empty. But on the way back to Shekar (or as it is now officially called: Sychar) the vessel will be sloshing and heavy. She knows every step of this route too well. Day in, day out, twice a day, at noon and then again after dusk. Water for washing, drinking, cooking, cleaning, always water. Water that she'll pull up, bucket after bucket, from the narrow well. The well that, according to history, was dug by her ancestor, Jacob. Jacob, with whom the bloody yet sacred history of Shekar began. This city that had become a bone of contention. Seized by a rival king an immeasurably long time ago. And since then, its inhabitants have worshipped on this mountain, and not in Jerusalem like the others. The others who revile them as traitors. As impure. As mixed race. Jerusalem, where they too keep the Scriptures of Moses and believe in Elohim.

Yes, Elohim. The God of heaven and of mountains. Or the God of Jerusalem. Jerusalem feels far away. Far from her worries. At home she has two little children and Shallum. No, of course not that famous Shallum, the Son of Jabesh and King of Samaria. Not a man from an important house. But a leather dealer from Caesarea, down by the sea. Business had led him here to the mountains, and it has been dragging on for some time now. At first he only came to her for one night. He paid the right price in copper coins. And then he found favour with her. Since then he has lived with her and given her money. And he isn't bad to her. At least if he's not drinking. But it's better than before. So much has happened since she ran away from Uri, her first husband, who had always beaten her. She moved from Shechem to the city. She lived with a new man, then subsequently changed partners for money. No, she is not a whore. Not really. But even if she was, who cares? She has two children at home. She doesn't quite know who their father is. But the mother, that much is certain.

Eventually she got used to the neighbours' sidelong looks. The women spitting in the street when she came by. Including women whose men, she knew, had come to her little mud hut on the edge of the city at night. The curses they throw after her – you, the sinner. And so she never washes her laundry with the others. That's why she never goes to the well when all the other women go there, in the morning, when it's cool. She walks alone and at noon when the oppressive heat makes every step difficult.

Ahead of her now, the last bend before the well. She knows it only too well, the shady green place around the stone-edged opening in the ground, from which the cool water is pulled in a vessel attached to a long winch. At first she does not notice him. The brown pitcher slides off her shoulder to the ground, she turns to the side. Startled, she pulls herself together. Here, directly to her right, sits a man on the bank of stones. Hastily, she covers her face and turns away. She prepares to be sent away. What does she want, a woman, if there is a man sitting here?

But suddenly, he speaks to her. He a man, she a woman, at a time when no one else is there. No one does such a thing! But that does not seem to bother him. He asks if she could give him a drink. There is something that almost sings in this voice, something free. Even the accent betrays him, the glimpse of the tassels on his white robe leaves no doubt: it is a Jew sitting in front of her. A man of thirty, maybe. He sits in front of her and looks her in the face. With his dark eyes in his fine face. A Jewish man, who appeals to her.

Something unheard of! But more than this, a Jew who asks for a drink! She cannot be hearing right!

How is this to be understood? He can see, surely, that she is a Samaritan. He even looks to her to be a scholar, a rabbi. A rabbi does not speak with an unknown woman. And if he knew the whole truth, how much less would he be willing to drink from her cup and become unclean, yes, even by giving her only a look?

'If you knew who I am and what the gift of God is, then you would have asked me, and I would have given you living water,' replies the mysterious stranger promptly. He speaks so strangely.

Living water? So not from a cistern, but running water? Here in the parched mountains of Samaria? How does that work? You haven't even got a vessel to draw with, and the well is deep. So where will you take this living water from? She smiles as the peculiar traveller looks at her so openly, and asks, 'Are you greater than our father Jacob, who dug this well?'

The cheeky question seems to amuse the rabbi. Now they both have to laugh. But in seconds he is back, the piercingly sharp but gentle look with the sound of these mysterious words. A sound that is so completely different to the way that other men speak. 'Whoever drinks of this water,' and with a slight inclination of the head, he points to the side of the well in the ground, 'Will thirst again later. But whoever drinks from the water that I will give them, will never thirst again; but the water that I give to them, in them will become a bubbling spring, whose waters are a fountain of eternal life.'

Eternal life? She almost wants to laugh again. She thinks of a pharmacist, who shouts in the market that he has a tincture to help cows become pregnant. Eternal life through plain water? What a devious promise! But nothing about the nature of this rabbi is devious. He speaks these words with the serenity of a man who knows what he is talking about. She has never heard more natural words. She returns his gaze, which is no longer playful. All her walls start to cave in. 'Lord, give me this water,' it comes spontaneously from her lips. Just what he's talking about, that's exactly what she wants. That's what she needs, and what she is looking for. Her eyes can't turn away from his. A long moment passes.

And with the same calm voice, the words that make time stand still. 'Go, call your husband.'

Bang! Your husband. Inwardly, she flinches like a roe deer, outwardly just her eyes register her embarrassment. A slight redness rises to her cheeks, half-concealed by the veil. Of a thousand questions he might have asked, and of thousands of subjects he could have addressed, it had to be that one. A bitter laugh rises inside. Your husband. Which one? The one she was once married to? The one she's living with now? All the others in between? Shame rises in her. This conversation started so well. But suddenly this. How dare he address her like this? What gives him the right? Fury burns in her stomach. But all this happens, lightning-quick, inside her. She has learned not to betray anything, and with a firm voice, in which only the slightest hint of a tremble betrays her inner emotion, she answers: 'I have no husband.'

Quite easily, these words have slipped from her lips. And yet now she lowers her eyes. Somehow, the initial magic of this brief encounter has given way to the oppression which she knows only too well. In her mind's eye now is Shallum. The stocky, black-bearded man with whom she shares the house. And then Uri, who renounced her. And Ariel, and all the others. 'I do not have a husband,' she says, shaking her head almost cynically; she feels so brazen. Suddenly she feels all the lies, all the confusion and all the wrong, and where her life has been stuck for so long.

But now, again, this singing in the voice of the stranger. So disarming and natural, as if a child were talking. 'You have spoken correctly. You do not have a husband. Because you had five men and the one you are living with is not your husband. So you have told the truth.'

She jerks upright and looks the man in the face. What? It shoots through her head, 'You have told the truth'? How can he talk like that? She feels so caught, so unmasked, so exposed. How does he know? Only now she feels how cheap it sounds: having had five men and now one who is not her husband. True. That's it. She feels naked, undressed, exposed. But exposed in the sight of pure grace. The truth? Did he really say I spoke the truth?! Well, that's one thing to call it. At least a small part of the truth! She can't fool this man; he shines through her heart like a lamp. But his word leaves her whole. He does not call her a liar. Here she sits. So completely seen but not convicted. A strange feeling. Somehow peaceful.

'Lord, I see you're a prophet,' she stammers. And all at once she can only think of God. To God you owe everything, she knows that. The God the Jews worship in Jerusalem and the God the Samaritans worship up here on the barren hill with its ancient, holy and disturbing legends. The God she feels so strange about. The God she cares about all of a sudden, with all the strength of her thirsty heart, now that she is speaking with this man here. How, yes, how should one worship God? The whole story of her people, their impact and all the holy and disturbing legends they have to forget. All this melts together under this question: how does one serve this God? And how can one cleanse oneself from sin before him? At which altar do you sacrifice to him, if you know how sinful you are?

Here speaks someone who knows what God is like. And he talks about him with the same assurance as he had earlier. 'Yet a time is coming and has now come when the true worshippers will worship the Father in the Spirit and in truth.' Stunned, she hangs on every word that comes from his lips. True worshipper? Such as these, the Father is looking for. Wait, God, a father? What is a father? She can hardly remember her own. The fathers of her children were also not so great. This man here is far too young to be her father. Looking at his brown eyes, however, his words seem so near and natural. From his mouth, this truth suddenly seems like the only thing that could ever be true. God is a father. Exactly that. And he is fatherly like this stranger. This man who treats her so differently from any man she has met before. He speaks like no other man and no earthly father ever has. 'Because the Father is looking for worshippers like these.' Jesus lowers his voice as if at the end of a long speech. The end of a search. Because she knows now that she herself is at the end of her search. Her long random walk. At the end of her thirst. She has arrived at the source. What she has longed for all her life. What she has been looking for in all the men and has not found. In the desperate wanderings, in the relationships and love affairs, which only left her thirstier. Can it really be true? The Father himself was looking for her. Today, the search is at an end. She will be found this noon, at Jacob's well. She finally comes home. And she becomes a worshipper.

Why is Jesus addressing this woman and her jumble of relationships? Why does he focus exactly on this sore spot? And how is it that this conversation about fetching water, related in the

I AM WHAT YOU ARE LOOKING FOR

fourth chapter of the Gospel of John, somehow begins and ends in worship? We have come to the end of this book. This book dealing with the question of learning to pray in twelve easy steps. The book that began with the question of what there was, if there was nothing. Not much was going on with this woman. She was alone at the well because the city did not want to know about her. Many relationships, but no man. Social outcast, scum. One of the rejected. And the only one at the well in the silence of noon, with her pitcher – there was nothing. But there was someone waiting for her. Waiting for her in the here and now and at the well. He was already there, only she had been elsewhere. He waited for her and started a conversation. He knew everything, but didn't condemn her. Of course he had to call out the point of her pain. No one is spared from the surrender. The confrontation with all the brokenness of one's own existence. But Jesus did not take advantage of this moment. He did not insist that the woman immediately clarified and changed her relationships. Apparently, it was enough to name the problem and to be in conversation about it. Even if she had nothing significant or presentable to report. Actually nothing. Exactly then, he was waiting for her in that very place.

Here, at the end of this book, it is the same for you. The father is looking for worshippers. Notice: he is not looking for adoration. He does not thirst for praise or rituals, but he is interested in real people who are not perfect, yet who stay

THE FATHER IS LOOKING FOR YOU.

and talk to him. They learn to worship him 'in Spirit and in truth' (John 4:23). Both in the spiritual dimension and in the reality of the here and now. And all of your own imperfections – they, too, are part of the truth. Here at the end of this book, you may also know this: the Father is looking for you. To know and to love him is your greatest and highest calling.

But what is the conclusion, what is the outlook and what happens next? All of the lessons of the last twelve chapters have had a single purpose: to help you to draw close to Jesus and stay close. This is exactly the essence of life as a Christian.

> *'As the Father has loved me, so have I loved you. Now remain in my love.'*
>
> JOHN 15:9

Jesus says this in that well-known speech about the vine, comparing us to the branches. Staying in Jesus, in his love, that's what it's about. He himself is the answer. He himself is the end of the search. We can't redeem ourselves in our own strength, and we can't become perfect on our own. It's all about relationship, not about performance. Isn't it an amazing truth that even though Jesus addressed a woman in a chaotic marriage situation, resolving the problem is not a prerequisite for a conversation about worship? Even her half-hearted, prettified version of the situation passed as truth. Jesus certainly has an opinion on marriage and sexuality. But all the power of change lies in talking to him, in staying in his love, whatever your 'sore point' is – and hopefully you have one! Hopefully you are not perfect, because then Jesus would not have come for you. He is a doctor for the sick, not the champion of the perfect (Matthew 9:12). Speak with him about it. Do not hide. Do not hide your sore spot. Please ask him for his opinion. Read what his word says. Stay in conversation. Stay in contact. Come back again and again to the place of encounter, the inner garden, the place at the well. All power lies in staying, in staying in the love of Jesus. In prayer. Just prayer. Prayer is not everything. But without prayer, it is all nothing.

ALL POWER LIES IN STAYING, IN STAYING IN THE LOVE OF JESUS.